HOT CONNECTIONS

JEWELRY

HOT CONNECTIONS JEWELRY

JEWELRY

THE COMPLETE SOURCEBOOK OF SOLDERING TECHNIQUES

JENNIFER CHIN

POTTER
CRAFT

NEW YORK

COVER ARTISTS/PHOTOGRAPHERS: FRONT (clockwise from top center): Jennifer Chin/Allen Bryan, Hilary Hachey/Hap Sakwa, Jennifer Chin/Allen Bryan, Lisa Crowder/Hap Sakwa, Donna Veverka/James Hall, Jennifer Chin/Allen Bryan. BACK: Jennifer Chin/Allen Bryan

PAGE 2: Earrings by Tami Rodrig. Sterling silver, paint, and resin. Photo by Robert Diamante
PAGE 4: Oval necklace by Donna D'Aquino. Sterling silver. Photo by Ralph Gabriner
PAGE 6: Bohemian set by Jennifer Chin. Sterling silver. Photo by Allen Bryan
PAGE 7: (left) Belt buckle by Laura Preshong. Sterling silver and blown glass. Photo by Allen Bryan; (right) Woven disc ring by Melissa Finelli. Sterling silver, 18K gold. Photo by Peter Harris
PAGE 9: Avocado ring by Hilary Hachey. Sterling silver. Photo by Hap Sakwa
PAGE 10: Rings by Donna D'Aquino. Sterling silver and 18K gold. Photo by Ralph Gabriner
PAGE 28: Lichen rings by Jennifer Chin. Sterling silver. Photo by Allen Bryan
PAGE 70: Circle in Circle earrings by Donna D'Aquino. Sterling silver. Photo by Robert Gabriner
PAGE 88: Fauna earrings by Jennifer Chin. Sterling silver. Photo by Allen Bryan
PAGE 108: Green Zulu bracelet by Lauren Schlossberg. Sterling silver and glass beads. Photo by Hap Sakwa
PAGE 130: Stairway necklace by Jennifer Chin. Sterling silver. Photo by Allen Bryan

Published in the United States by Potter Craft, an imprint of the Crown Publishing Group, a division of Random House, Inc., New York.
www.crownpublishing.com
www.pottercraft.com

POTTER CRAFT and colophon is a registered trademark of Random House, Inc.

Library of Congress Cataloging-in-Publication Data
Chin, Jennifer.
  Hot connections jewelry : the complete sourcebook of soldering techniques / Jennifer Chin. — 1st ed.
    p. cm.
  Includes index.
  ISBN 978-0-8230-3336-2 (pbk.)
  1. Jewelry making. 2. Solder and soldering. I. Title.
  TT212.C495 2011
  739.27--dc22

                                        2010038622

DESIGN by Laura Palese

ILLUSTRATIONS by Cathy Chin

LESSON AND PROJECT PHOTOGRAPHY by Christopher McGillicuddy

Printed in China

10 9 8 7 6 5 4 3 2 1

First Edition

ACKNOWLEDGMENTS

To my ever-supportive and patient husband, who over the years has played several roles in my jewelry career: studio assistant, roadie, graphic designer, photographer, and Eagle Scout, to name a few. I could not have done this without you. Thank you for your deep understanding, friendship, and love.

Thanks to all my beloved friends and family for their support and help. Thank you, Mom, for your beautiful illustrations. I see your hand in each drawing, which makes this book a very special collaboration. Thank you to my editor, Joy Aquilino, who had unwavering faith in and encouragement for this first-time author. Thank you to my fabulous contributing artists, whose jewelry elevates this book to a higher level. It's an honor to include your work, which is an inspiration to me and to newcomers to our craft.

CONTENTS

PREFACE

Working with metal is a pleasure. Its versatility and malleability allow for endless creative possibilities. I began working with sterling silver and gold a decade ago, and my love of metalworking only continues to grow. The process of making metal jewelry—tactile, symbolic, decorative, and primal—fulfills many physical and emotional needs for me. There's something very satisfying about heating metal with fire and working it into a beautiful form.

I conceived of *Hot Connections Jewelry* as an easy-to-follow resource for people who have experience making jewelry with beading, wirework, or cold-connection techniques and want to expand their skills to include soldering in their creative repertoires. This book is unique in that it provides a wide-ranging yet detailed survey of a variety of techniques that use a torch and solder. I offer guidance about setting up a workspace, buying a torch, and choosing and using some essential tools. In addition to soldering, I cover basic fabrication techniques, such as sawing, filing, and riveting, as well as more advanced techniques like creating surface textures, setting stones, and using inlay. *Hot Connections Jewelry* also includes twenty-three lessons and fifteen projects, each of which builds upon skills taught previously by incorporating a new technique. The projects can be copied exactly or used as inspiration to create unique designs. Each chapter is supplemented with photographs of my own jewelry as well as that of other jewelers, so you can see the range of creative outcomes that are possible with these techniques. This blend of reference and inspiration is designed to answer the many questions asked by jewelry makers who are new to soldering—questions I had when I was a beginner. There are, of course, many different aspects and tangents within every technique and too many variations to include in one book. I encourage you to further pursue any technique that interests you and experiment; it's the best way to learn about the tools and materials.

Before you begin soldering, I'd like to offer some advice: First, there's no one "correct" way to make jewelry, only techniques that provide direction and encourage experimentation with tools and materials. If you're new to soldering, I encourage you to try the projects, use different materials, and explore the possibilities. The saying "Learn from your mistakes" definitely applies here; every experience is valuable, and some of the best ideas come about through happy accident. Second, remember that a good design is nothing if the quality is shoddy: You not only want to enjoy making your creations but to be proud of them, too. For many jewelers, it's the process as well as the end product that make metalwork so meaningful. Have fun, and good luck!

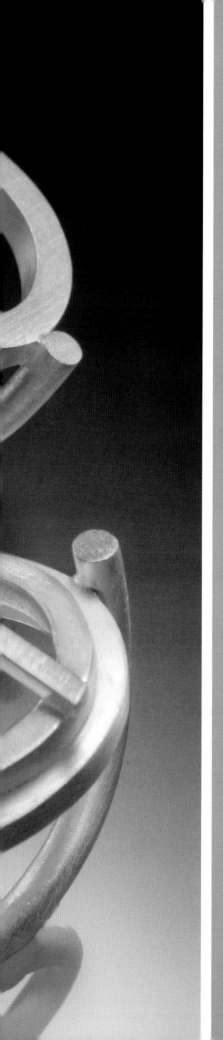

1

SOLDERING

BASICS

HOW SOLDERING WORKS

Although it's possible to create jewelry from separate units, such as beads and wire, being able to permanently join—or solder—metal components can greatly further your creativity, versatility, and confidence in jewelry making. Soldering calls for a combination of scientific understanding and perception; at the same time, it's a simple process of heating, timing, and observation. It is a skill anyone can master with practice.

While successful soldering is best learned through experience, some basic knowledge of its physics is helpful. Soldering (more correctly called *silver brazing*) is the method of joining metals using an alloy (solder) that has been heated to a fluid state. The molten solder is distributed between a joint by capillary action. At its liquefied temperature, the molten solder interacts with a thin layer of the base metal, cooling to form a sealed,

invisible seam. A good solder joint should be as strong as the piece as a whole. Tools used in soldering processes include a torch to heat the metals, various tweezers and picks used to apply solder and hold components in place, and a fireproof work surface. For solder to successfully join metals, a chemical called *flux* must be used to keep the metals clean. Surface oxidation occurs when metal is heated. This oxidation inhibits proper solder flow, as the metal must remain clean for the solder to flow into a joint. After soldering, metals need to be cleaned of the surface residue left by the flux, which, when cool, becomes hard like glass. *Pickle* is a strong acid solution that will remove the flux and oxides. To work effectively, the pickle solution must be warm and is best kept in a heating container, such as a Crock-Pot. All of these elements and processes will be discussed further throughout the book.

EARRINGS BY DONNA VEVERKA,
sterling silver and gold bi-metal

These earrings were all created using basic fabrication techniques, including piercing, annealing, forming, and soldering.
PHOTO BY JAMES HULL

METALS

Each type of metal exhibits unique qualities when heated, forged, soldered, and finished, which can make working with any metal a challenge—but one with excellent payoffs. Many jewelers work with nonferrous metals (metals that don't contain iron), which include base metals, precious metals, and alloys; the most popular of these are discussed below. Most of the projects in this book use sterling silver, a relatively inexpensive alloy, but I encourage beginners to start with even less-expensive base metals, such as copper and alloys such as brass and nickel silver, which yield great results for most processes.

NONPRECIOUS METALS

Nonprecious metals, often referred to as base metals, are commonly found nonferrous metals. Ferrous metals are metals containing iron. Copper, lead, nickel, and zinc oxidize quickly and are often used in industrial applications, as they conduct heat and electricity well. Base metal alloys include brass, bronze, and nickel silver. These alloys, including copper, are often used in decorative arts, as they can be easily cut, formed, melted, and used in casting. Here are a few inexpensive base metals that can be used for any of the book's lessons or projects.

COPPER

Copper was one of the earliest metals to be found and used by humans, and it is still one of the most widely used, as it conducts heat and electricity and combines well with many other metals to create a large range of alloys. Newly mined copper is actually a pink or peach-colored metal. In part because its hardness is similar to that of sterling silver, copper is an excellent practice material for making jewelry since it can be sawed, bent, formed, and soldered in the same manner as sterling. Copper has a melting point of 1981°F (1082°C) and can be oxidized with heat to create beautiful colors.

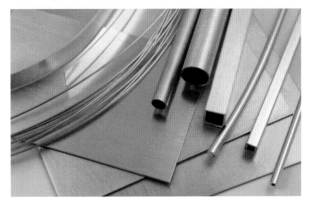

The various metals, from left to right: sterling and fine silver wire, sterling silver, brass and copper sheet, and various types of sterling silver and gold tubing.

BRASS

An alloy of copper and zinc, brass has a muted yellow color somewhat similar to gold and is relatively resistant to tarnishing. It's available in several variations: In addition to Nu-Gold (88% copper and 12% zinc), which is an excellent practice jewelry material and stand-in for gold, there are many others used for jewelry making. Higher-zinc brasses are often used to make screws, fittings, musical instruments, and plumbing applications. Brass has a melting point within a range of 1600°F (871°C) to 2000°F (1093°C).

BRONZE

Bronze is an alloy of copper and tin. Other elements sometimes added to bronze include phosphorus, manganese, aluminum, and silicon. Bronze is often used in casting because it melts easily and is less corrosive than copper or steel. This quality is key to sculpture or artwork that is exposed to elements that cause rapid surface oxidation. It has a melting point within a range of 1900°F (1037°C) to 1950°F (1065°C).

NICKEL SILVER

Despite its name, nickel silver contains no silver at all but is actually an alloy of copper, nickel, and zinc. It has a yellowish-gray color that's similar to white gold. Nickel silver is a great practice material, because it can be soldered, forged, and polished similarly to copper and silver. Nickel silver has a melting point of 1959°F (1070°C).

PRECIOUS METALS

Gold, silver, and platinum are nonferrous metals considered to be precious metals due to their rarity and beauty. Gold and platinum, though lovely to work with, are very expensive and not appropriate for beginning jewelers. Most of the lessons and projects in the book use sterling silver as the material, as it's generally affordable and wonderful to work with.

GOLD

Gold is one of the most highly prized metals. Used for coinage, jewelry, and decoration, gold is known for its extreme malleability and shiny, warm glow. This soft metal won't tarnish, can be polished to a high luster, and mixes well to create a wide variety of alloys. Its density and resistance to oxidation make it well suited for use as a protective coating over other, reactive metals. Gold's melting point varies from 1515°F (823°C) to 2300°F (1260°C).

SILVER

Silver is a white metal that, like unalloyed gold, is very soft. Not to be confused with sterling silver (an alloy of silver and copper), pure or "fine" silver is often used in the creation of bezels, which are soft rims of metal that hold stones in a setting. Silver is also used in enameling, as its softness and resistance to tarnishing are useful. Its melting point is 1761°F (960°C).

PLATINUM

Platinum is a lustrous, dark silver metal that's more costly than gold. It is extremely durable and malleable and often used in settings for diamonds and other precious stones. Its resistance to corrosion and its high melting point make it well suited for use in laboratory and industrial equipment. An oxygen-fed torch must be used when working with platinum because of its high melting point. There are many by-products of platinum ore: palladium, rhodium, and iridium to name a few. Platinum has a melting point of 3225°F (1773°C).

ALLOYS

Because precious metals such as gold and silver are, in their pure states, too soft to be practical for most jewelry making, they can be strengthened by combination with one or more other metals to create an alloy. In addition to being more durable than a pure metal, an alloy may also have a desirable color or lower melting point. Solders (see page 52) are also alloys; silver solder, for example, is an alloy of silver and zinc.

STERLING SILVER

Sterling silver is an alloy of 92.5% silver and 7.5% copper. The mixture of these two metals results in an alloy with silver's characteristic bright shine but with more strength; the downside is that the copper oxidizes (reacts with oxygen in the air) to form tarnish. Firescale (see page 58) is also an issue when working with sterling silver. The melting point of sterling silver is 1640°F (893°C).

MELTING POINTS OF VARIOUS METALS

METAL	SYMBOL	MELTING POINT
BRASS	70/30	1750°F (954°C)
COPPER	Cu	1981°F (1083°C)
GOLD	Au	1945°F (1063°C)
NICKEL	Ni	2651°F (1453°C)
PLATINUM	Pt	3224°F (1773°C)
SILVER	Ag	1761°F (960.5°C)
STERLING SILVER	925	1640°F (893°C)

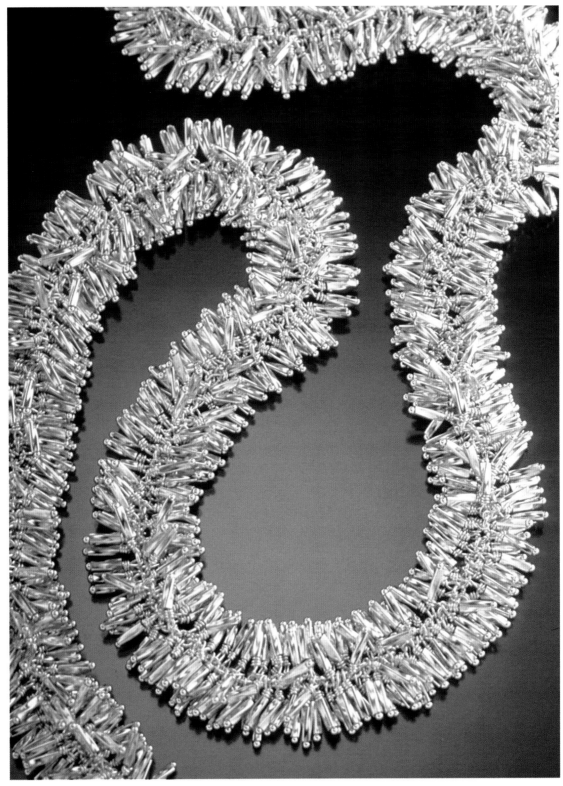

SHAG NECKLACE BY JENNIFER CHIN, *sterling and fine silver*

I used fine silver wire to create tiny pins, which were then used to thread and wire-wrap the beads to a chain. Fine silver is much more pliable than sterling, making the wire-wrapping process easier. **PHOTO BY ALLEN BRYAN**

GOLD ALLOYS

The amount (or fraction) of pure gold in an alloy is called its *karat* (not to be confused with the term *carat*, which is a unit of weight for gemstones). The karat of gold is measured in 24 parts. For example, the ratio of 18-karat gold is 18/6 (gold/alloy), whereas pure gold is 24/0.

There are several alloys that are color variations of gold. Each alloy is malleable and lovely to work with. White gold is made by adding nickel or palladium to pure gold. Nickel white gold is tough to work with, as it's very hard and tends to create firescale on workpieces. Palladium white gold is much easier to work with; it has a higher melting point than yellow gold, is softer, and leaves no firescale on its surface. The most common gold alloy, yellow gold is created by adding silver and copper to pure gold. Rose or pink gold results from the addition of copper to gold, which gives the metal a slight redness. Green gold is created by adding silver, cadmium, and zinc to pure gold. The melting points and properties of these alloys vary depending on the percentages of the metals added.

GOLD-FILLED

The terms "gold-filled," "rolled gold," and "rolled gold plate" are used to describe a base metal (usually brass) that has a thin layer of gold fused to its surface. The gold is soldered to the surface, then drawn or flattened. Gold-filled wire should never be heated or soldered. It's most useful in the creation of (unsoldered) jump rings and earring wires.

PURCHASING METALS

Metals for jewelry making are manufactured in many forms, including sheets, wire, and tubing. Purchasing metals in premade forms can save time and handwork, though the cost may be higher. Round, square, rectangular, and triangular wire can be found in many different gauges, or thicknesses. Tubing in assorted shapes is also a time-saving material that can spur design creativity.

The thickness of metal sheet and wire is often measured using the Brown & Sharpe, or B & S, measurement system. A B & S wire-and-sheet gauge is a handy tool to have when making measurements. The lower the number, the thicker the sheet or wire. Precious metals are also measured in troy ounces or penny weights.

BROWN & SHARPE (B & S) GAUGES

BROWN & SHARPE GAUGE	INCHES	MILLIMETERS
2	0.257	6.52
4	0.204	5.18
6	0.162	4.11
8	0.128	3.24
10	0.101	2.57
12	0.080	2.03
14	0.064	1.63
16	0.050	1.27
18	0.040	1.02
20	0.031	0.79
22	0.025	0.64
24	0.020	0.51
26	0.015	0.38
28	0.012	0.30
30	0.010	0.25

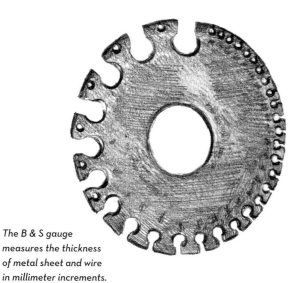

The B & S gauge measures the thickness of metal sheet and wire in millimeter increments.

OPPOSITE: HONEYCOMB NECKLACE BY JENNIFER CHIN, *sterling silver Made entirely from sterling silver, this necklace makes extensive use of jump rings (covered more on page 43) as an integral part of the design.* **PHOTO BY ALLEN BRYAN**

CHOOSING TORCHES & GASES

For soldering operations, you must have a torch to produce a flame. A torch combines air or oxygen with a gas and is lit to produce a flame hot enough to heat and solder metals. There are many options for producing a soldering flame, from small handheld butane torches to more advanced oxy-acetylene systems. Choosing a torch will depend on what kind of soldering operations you want to achieve and what you're comfortable with.

The most popular gases used by jewelers are acetylene, propane, and butane, all of which can be purchased in refillable tanks through welding supply companies. Included in a torch kit is a hand piece with adjustable knobs for controlling flame size, torch tips, and a pressure valve called a regulator, which provides fixed pressure (releasing the gas from the tank at a constant pressure). The regulator is necessary, as the gas inside the tank is under a huge amount of pressure when filled to maximum capacity. One of the main differences between torch types is the source of oxygen used to support combustion. Acetylene ambient-air torches have a single knob and hose and use the oxygen in the air instead of a separate tank of pure oxygen. The result is a "dirtier" flame that will not get as hot as an oxygen-fed flame, but it works well when soldering base metals, sterling silver, and gold. (The term *dirtier* refers to a flame that creates more surface oxidation on the metal being worked.) This torch is excellent for situations and environments in which tanks of oxygen are restricted, such as in apartments and urban areas.

Note the hoses of this oxy-acetylene mini torch: red for fuel and green for oxygen.

VARIOUS TORCH TYPES

TORCH	FUEL	TEMPERATURE	EASE OF USE
LITTLE/MINI TORCH	Acetylene/Oxygen	3500°F (1926°C)	somewhat easy
LITTLE/MINI TORCH	Propane/Oxygen	2500°F (1400°C)	somewhat easy
ATMOSPHERIC TORCH	Acetylene/Air	1700°F (972°C)	easy
BUTANE MICRO TORCH	Butane	2500°F (1371°C)	easy

Oxy-acetylene or oxy-propane torches use pure oxygen with acetylene or propane. They have separate knobs and hoses for the two tanks: a red hose for fuel and a green hose for oxygen. Flames produced from these pure-oxygen torches are hotter than atmosphere-using torches, because the ambient air only contains roughly 20% oxygen, the rest being nitrogen and carbon dioxide, which aren't useful for burning. Oxygen-fed torches are necessary for soldering metals with high melting points, such as platinum.

The "little" or "mini" torch is an excellent choice for beginners. Disposable oxygen and propane gas tanks are readily available at hardware stores and welding supply companies and are better for those who prefer not to store large tanks in the home. This style of torch comes with interchangeable tips and lets the user easily control oxygen flow and flame size.

Less intimidating butane "micro" torches are ideal for beginners, too, as they're inexpensive and require no large tanks of fuel or oxygen. Self-contained and handheld, butane torches have push-button igniters and a delicate, adjustable flame, allowing you to work with small pieces, such as jump rings and earring wires. The micro torch can hold between 5 and 30 grams of butane, depending on the model, and has a burning time of around 35 minutes. Reaching a temperature of 2500°F (1400°C), commercial butane torches will work with many of the projects in this book.

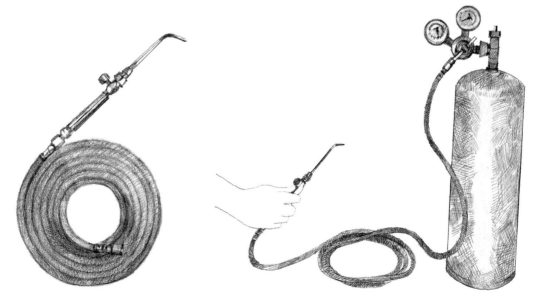

Acetylene torch alone (left) and attached to a tank (right).

FLAME TYPES

Adjusting the amount of fuel fed into a torch controls the heat in a flame. A larger flame isn't necessarily hotter. A flame fed with a higher amount of oxygen may be small but can be much hotter than an ambient-air-fed flame. Manually controlling the mix with atmospheric and butane torches isn't possible, as they only have one knob; instead, the flame is controlled by air-intake holes that let in just enough air to balance with the gas coming out of the tank. Turning up the gas will cause the torch to suck in more air to balance the mix. With oxygen-fed torches, you can control the mix manually.

The most commonly used soldering flame type is a *neutral flame* (one in which the mixture of gas and oxygen is balanced). A *reducing flame* is created with more fuel than oxygen in the mix. A bushy flame is used to reduce surface oxidation, for annealing, for depletion gilding, and for melting silver and gold. A flame with too much oxygen in the mix is called an *oxidizing flame,* which is not useful for metalsmithing. It produces a high-pitched hissing sound and a pale flame.

In addition, different flame types exhibit different *flame cones.* The term *cone* refers to the flame's shape. A soldering flame is wide and round at the mouth of the torch and tapers to a point at the flame's tip. For example, neutral flames have an outer blue cone with an inner white cone where the acetylene and oxygen combine. The tip of the inner white cone is the hottest point of the flame.

IGNITING AND EXTINGUISHING TORCHES

The steps for lighting and turning off various torch types are outlined below. But regardless of torch type, when preparing to light a torch, the following safety precautions always apply: *Always secure gas tanks so that they cannot tip over.* My tank is tightly strapped to my workbench table leg. Check each junction of your torch for leaks; a soapy-water solution painted over a joint will bubble if there's any leakage. Don't overtighten torch fittings, because this may ruin the threading and impair fit. And be aware of the smell of fuel, indicating a leak. If there is a leak, disconnect your torch immediately, and put the leaking tank outside to be removed.

OXY-ACETYLENE OR OXY-PROPANE MINI TORCH

1 The pressure on your gas tanks should be between 5 and 10 psi (pound-force per square inch). Turn the knob on the acetylene or propane regulator about one-eighth of a turn counterclockwise to begin the gas flow from the tank; the psi should not change, since the regulator is providing a fixed-pressure release of the gas.

2 Using a striker (tool for igniting a torch flame), ignite the gas at the tip of the torch. (See image B, opposite.)

3 Slowly turn the oxygen regulator knob in a counter-clockwise direction, allowing a small amount of oxygen into the flame. Keep turning the oxygen knob to achieve a colorless inner cone (the hottest part of the flame) with a dark blue outer cone. This is a neutral flame, the one most commonly used for soldering throughout this book.

4 When shutting off this torch, always turn off the oxygen first and then the gas.

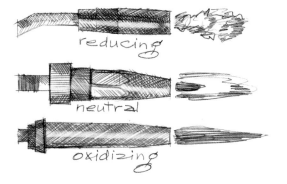

Different types of flames will look different, as this illustrations shows.

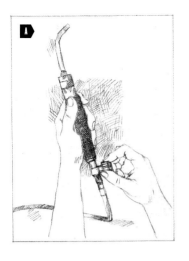

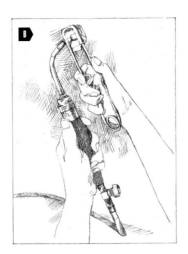

ACETYLENE AMBIENT-AIR TORCH

1 Turn the knob counterclockwise about one-eighth of a turn (A). There should be no hissing gas sound.

2 Using your striker (also see page 54), ignite the gas at the tip of the torch (B).

3 Turn the knob counterclockwise slowly to adjust your flame's size (C). As this is a single-hose torch using

ambient air, it isn't possible to control the amount of oxygen fed to the flame. A bigger flame must be used when more heat is needed. Large pieces, heavy-gauge wire, or thick metal (such as that used for ring bands) require a bigger flame for even heating. A smaller flame should be used for more delicate work (such as earring wires and chains).

4 Turn off the torch by turning the knob clockwise.

BUTANE MICRO TORCH

1 There are many different models available, so be sure to read your torch's instructions thoroughly.

2 Turn on the key switch to let out the gas, and then push the igniter button to light the flame.

3 To adjust the flame, turn the key switch; turning it counterclockwise will reduce flame size.

4 To turn off the torch, turn the key switch all the way counterclockwise.

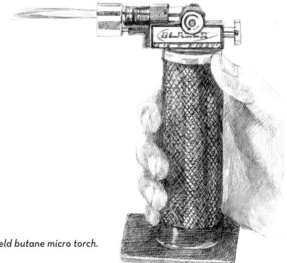

A handheld butane micro torch.

SETTING UP A WORKSPACE

A jeweler's bench can be set up almost anywhere. Some people work in their basements or a compact area of their living space. Others choose to rent an entire workspace outside the home. Before setting up your work area, you should consider key factors, such as proper lighting, ventilation, and availability of such resources as electrical outlets and a sink. To take good care of your equipment, it's a good idea to relegate areas for certain tasks—for example, areas for hot and cold techniques or wet and dry tasks. In my studio, I have a jeweler's bench and several worktables where I have a fabrication area, a soldering station, and a cleaning/finishing table. As not much space is generally needed, soldering, fabrication, and cleaning areas can share a worktable if your space is limited; just be sure to keep metal tools away from water and pickle. For beginning jewelers, a sturdy, well-lit table with a bench pin (see page 32), nearby sink, and good ventilation make for a fine workspace.

ESSENTIAL WORKBENCH TOOLS

The following are tools you'll need for various jewelry-making processes.
Pages are referenced where these techniques are discussed in greater depth.

CUTTING & PIERCING
(see pages 32, 36, and 38)

Jeweler's saw frame

Saw blades
(in sizes 1, 1/0, 2/0)

Bench pin

Hand files
(flat, round, square, half-round, and barrette)

Needle files
(flat, round, square, half-round, and barrette)

Beeswax or Bur-Life blade lubricant

Cutters (flush and compound)

Shears

Flexible shaft with drill bits

HOLDING
(see pages 33 and 54)

Bench vise

Tweezers

Tube cutter

TEXTURE & FINISHING
(see pages 40 and 90)

Brass and steel brushes

Sandpaper
(assortment of 220–400 grit)

Various burrs and drill bits

MEASURING
(see page 31)

Calipers

Rulers

Scribe

FORMING
(see pages 41, 45, 74, 76, and 90)

Pliers
(needle-nose, flat-nose, and round-nose)

Mallets
(rawhide and plastic)

Chasing hammer

Riveting hammer

Ball-peen hammer

Planishing hammer

Steel block

Steel ring and bezel mandrels

Anvil

Wood block or stump

Chasing stamps and punches

Dapping block and punches

Flaring tool

SAFETY
(see page 24)

Safety glasses and gloves

Ear protection

Ventilator

NONESSENTIAL BUT USEFUL
(see page 94)

Rolling mill

My workbench: On the left is a jeweler's bench where I do my fabrication. To the right is my soldering station.

BASIC SOLDERING TOOL KIT

As we move through the soldering processes and lessons, the equipment will be discussed in greater depth, but the following list outlines all the basics that you'll need.

Soldering torch with fuel source, regulator, and assorted sizes of tips

Striker

Soldering surfaces (firebricks, charcoal blocks, and ceramic tiles)

Tweezers

Locking tweezers

Soldering pick

Flux

Small brush (for applying flux)

Solder (hard, medium, and easy)

Cutters or snips for cutting wire solder

Shears for cutting sheet solder

Pickle

Pickle pot or Crock-Pot

Copper tongs

Binding wire

Third hand

Water for quenching

Safety glasses

Fire extinguisher

SAFE VENTILATION

When choosing a work area, consider the air quality and how it may affect the rest of your home. Heating and soldering create hazardous fumes and smoke. Wear a respirator, or create a ventilated work area with a simple vented stove hood above the soldering area that vents out a window. You can make another do-it-yourself vent at the back of your soldering area with a Shop-Vac with a PVC pipe attached to the hose. Drill a series of holes in the PVC pipe to create an air-intake vent, and lay the PVC tube along the back edge of your soldering area.

RESPIRATOR TIPS

- ▢ Be sure the respirator has the proper filter for the chemicals to which you'll be exposed.
- ▢ Fit is key. Your mask must be airtight but comfortable to wear.
- ▢ Change filters as needed.
- ▢ Dust masks are not sufficient protection from fumes.

Soldering respirator with filters and an adjustable strap.

This simple ventilation system was created with a fan, aluminum ducts, and connectors to vent soldering fumes to the outside.

SAFETY GOGGLES

You should always wear plastic safety goggles during any metalworking processes. Eyeglasses are not sufficient protection. I recommend wearing eye protection while soldering or when using any machinery. In addition to protecting your eyes, skin, and lungs, you should also protect your ears, which are at risk while forging and hammering. Wear earplugs or large, padded headphones to protect your eardrums from loud shop noise.

Safety equipment such as respirators, goggles, and headphones are available through jewelry and welding supply companies (see Resources). Many hardware stores also carry safety equipment, such as dust masks and rubber gloves.

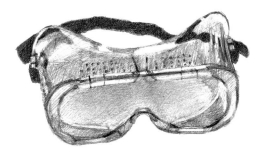

Plastic safety goggles with an adjustable strap can be found at any jeweler's supply retailer or hardware store.

PREPARING A WORK SURFACE FOR SOLDERING

Line the surface of your worktable with ceramic tiles or firebricks to create a solid heat barrier. There are many soldering surfaces available, including asbestos-free pads, charcoal blocks, honeycomb ceramic blocks, and pumice-filled pans. It's entirely up to you which surface you find works best for each soldering job, but it's good to have a few options on hand. Never set up your workstation near flammable objects or chemicals. Be sure to have a sink or bowl of cool water nearby at all times.

Charcoal blocks, soldering boards, and pebble-filled soldering trays (from top to bottom, above) all create fireproof protection for your worktable surface.

SAFETY CONSIDERATIONS

- ☐ Always wear eye and ear protection.
- ☐ Use gloves when handling chemicals.
- ☐ Long hair and loose clothing can easily be caught in machinery, so be sure to tie back anything that could catch.
- ☐ Label and store chemicals properly, and keep them in a secure location away from children and pets.
- ☐ Wear an apron while working to protect your clothes from spills and splashes.
- ☐ Be sure your workspace is ventilated. An open window is not enough to vent fumes.
- ☐ Keep a fire extinguisher in an easily accessible place.

GETTING STARTED USING A TORCH

One of the first basic techniques that can be done with a torch is annealing, so even though it isn't soldering, it's a good technique to explore here with a first lesson to gain familiarity with using your torch. Annealing is the process of heating metal to soften and prepare it for further work, such as shaping, stamping, or forming. You can do this either with a torch or in a kiln.

At room temperature, metals exist on a molecular level as crystals in variously shaped units. Heating the metal evenly and slowly with a torch causes the atoms in its crystalline structure to spread apart, making the metal softer and more malleable. When the metal is hammered, rolled, filed, or otherwise worked when soft, the large crystals are broken into smaller ones; this is called *work-hardening*. Thin ear wires can be hardened by gently twisting the posts using pliers. If there's no easy way to work-harden the metal, you can use the technique of *age-hardening*. To do this, place your workpiece in a preheated oven set at 526°F for 2½ hours.

Different metals anneal at different temperatures. Color changes in the metal are the indicator that the correct annealing temperature has been achieved. By moving the torch over the metal and observing the change in color, one can see when metal is properly annealed. When learning to anneal, working in low light is helpful, as color changes can be more easily seen. Certain metals must be quenched in water after heating to achieve proper annealing, while some need to air cool. Silver, gold, copper, and nickel share the same crystal structures, making their pliability similar when annealed.

ABOVE: BARBELL NECKLACES BY JENNIFER CHIN, *sterling silver*

These round elements were created by annealing, forming, soldering, and hammering flat wire. The connecting elements were created by soldering hollow beads to the ends of round wire.
PHOTO BY ALLEN BRYAN

ANNEALING COLOR INDICATION

FOR METALS TO BE QUENCHED IN WATER AFTER HEATING:

☐ Sterling silver and copper: Heat to dull red.

☐ 18K to 22K yellow gold: Heat to very dark red.

☐ 14K gold: Heat to dark red.

☐ Fine silver and 24K gold: Heat to black.

FOR METALS THAT AIR COOL AFTER HEATING:

☐ White nickel-based gold and brass: Heat to bright red.

Annealing of metals usually occurs *after* soldering, but again, this lesson serves as an introduction to using the torch. I'm using sterling silver here, but you can choose any metal to practice this technique.

WHAT YOU'LL NEED

Basic soldering tool kit (see page 23)
Your choice of metal
Bowl of water

1 Working in a dimly lit area, place your metal on a charcoal block or other fireproof surface.

2 Light your torch, and adjust it to a large, bushy flame.

3 Heat the metal evenly until it is glowing and dull red, if using silver (A). Check the box on the opposite page for proper annealing colors of other metals.

4 Using tongs, quench the metal in water.

5 Your metal is now prepared to be bent, forged, or hammered.

A

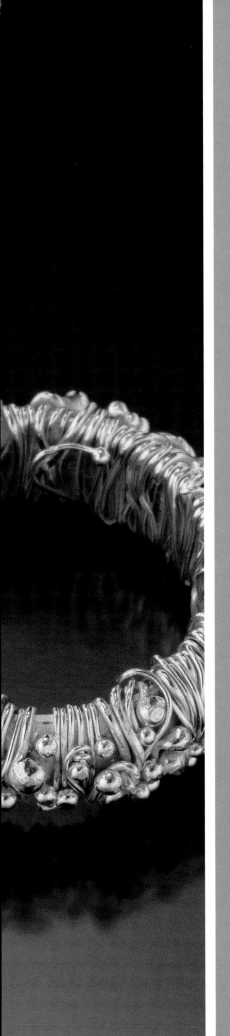

2

ESSENTIAL
FABRICATION

& SOLDERING TECHNIQUES

BASIC FABRICATION OVERVIEW

Fabrication is generally the first step when working with metals. Before beginning to solder, you must go through many steps of basic fabrication to prepare your metals first. Cutting, piercing, filing, and forming are just a few techniques of basic fabrication. It's important to master these processes, as they're the cornerstone of any jewelry-making project, and for better or worse, the first step will affect those that follow.

What follows in this chapter are discussions of various jewelry-fabrication techniques and the tools needed for them. Like choosing clothing, buying tools is a personal act; in the end, you buy what you're comfortable with, depending on price and need. Sometimes it's important to invest in a pricier tool to get the best results, but often, a cheaper product will serve your needs just as well. I've spent years adding to my tool collection. Some pieces are used once a month, some on a daily basis. It's up to you to choose what tools you need, but this chapter covers some basic pieces every jeweler needs.

SWAN EARRINGS BY LISA CROWDER, *sterling silver*

These earrings were created using the basic fabrication techniques of dapping and forming. **PHOTO BY HAP SAKWA**

MEASURING

Layout and measurement tools are essential for quality jewelry making. Components that don't fit together properly can cause problems throughout a piece's creation. To save yourself a lot of grief, be sure your first measurements are precise. I use my B & S wire gauge, small steel ruler, and scribe on a daily basis. Other useful measuring devices include calipers for precise measurements and divider calipers, which are used to measure a distance between two points.

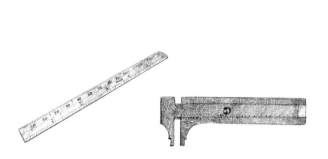 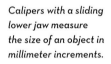  

A small steel ruler is used to make measurements and create straight lines with a scribe.

Calipers with a sliding lower jaw measure the size of an object in millimeter increments.

Divider calipers measure the distance between two points.

Used with a hammer, a center punch creates a divot in metal. Divots serve as starting points for drill bits when drilling holes. Placing the drill bit in the divot keeps the bit in place (where you want the hole to be), preventing it from skidding or sliding across the metal surface.

A scribe is a sharp tool used to etch shallow marks and guidelines in a metal surface before cutting, bending, and so on.

Here, the scribe is being used with a ruler to "draw" a straight guideline. A guideline can be created for many operations—for example, to saw along when you want to make a straight cut, for bending, or for filing.

SAWING & CUTTING

When beginning a jewelry project, the first step is often cutting or sawing. Jewelers often purchase metals in raw form, most commonly as sheet or wire. To use these metals, components must be cut from the sheet, or segments must be cut from the wire. As they are generally a first step, sawing and cutting are essential techniques for a successful outcome.

SAW FRAME AND BLADES

In my studio, nothing gets more daily action than my saw frame. It's one of the most versatile tools on any jeweler's workbench. Saw frames are sold in different depths. Larger saw frames are useful when cutting large sheets of metal, smaller saw frames for cutting tubing and wire. Purchasing a high-quality saw frame is important, because cheap saw frames can cause blade breakage, which wastes time and money.

Jeweler's saw blades come in 6-inch lengths and are available in seventeen sizes of varying thicknesses. The smallest is 8/0, and the largest is 8. I use a 2/0 in my daily work and in the projects in this book. For added ease while sawing and piercing, use Bur-Life or beeswax lubricants with saw blades, drill bits, and hand files.

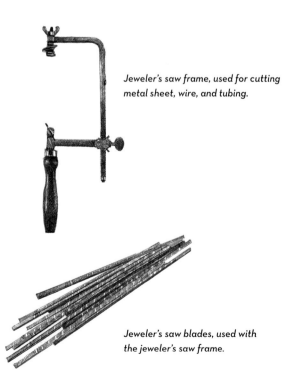

Jeweler's saw frame, used for cutting metal sheet, wire, and tubing.

Jeweler's saw blades, used with the jeweler's saw frame.

BENCH PIN

A bench pin is an essential tool used for more successful sawing, filing, and support and ease of motion during many jewelry-making techniques. It's a simple block of wood firmly fixed to a workbench; the shape may vary to suit individual needs. You can buy a premade pin from any jeweler's supply company (see Resources) or make your own by cutting a V shape like the one shown below out of a 4 x 6–inch piece of wood, approximately ½-inch thick, and drilling some holes for attaching screws. The screw holes should be located opposite the V side of the wood block. Drill the holes a ½-inch in from the end, and secure the pin to the edge of your worktable. The bench pin should extend out at least 5½ inches from the edge of the table. Mount the bench pin at chest level (when you're seated) on your workbench for best results.

You can always alter the bench pin to suit your needs; cut or file it as desired. Many jewelers also use a large piece of leather hung below the bench pin like a hammock to catch filings and scrap pieces.

A bench pin with steel block. This style of bench pin is attached to a worktable with a portable clamp and incorporates a handy steel block surface for hammering along with the bench pin.

HOLDING TOOLS

Holding tools are excellent devices used to hold objects in place while they're being cut, filed, set, and hammered. A small bench vise securely mounted to your worktable is helpful for holding metal steady while it's worked, filed, or bent into right angles. One of my favorite tools is the tube cutter; it's an invaluable device with an adjustable-length extender used to hold tubing and wire while cutting. Used with a jeweler's saw, it's excellent for making repeated straight cuts and creating many segments of the same length.

SNIPS AND SHEARS

Cutting tools—such as flush cutters, snips, and shears—are invaluable for cutting wire, bezel wire, thin gauges of sheet metal, and solder. Have several on hand, including a flush cutter for making straight-edged cuts and a sturdier pair for cutting wire and thicker metal. Shears are useful when cutting tiny squares of sheet solder and trimming thin sheet metal from the edges around bezels.

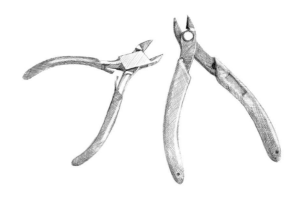

Mini bench vise with a revolving action. Used for holding metal while it's being worked, this vise rotates and tilts for added maneuverability. Vises can be purchased through jeweler's supply companies and hardware stores, as can most other necessary tools.

A cutter (shown left) is used to snip wires, solder, and so on. It creates an angled, or a pinched, edge on the wire when it cuts. Regular cutters are useful for cutting through thick wire. A flush cutter (shown right) creates a flat edge and is useful for cutting ends of bezel wire and wire that needs a flat end.

Tube-cutting jig. This handy tool is perfect for making adjustable, precise cuts in tubing, rods, and wire.

Cutting shears are used for cutting thin sheet metal and are handy for making smooth, even curves.

USING A JEWELER'S SAW

Successful sawing can be achieved with patience and practice. Here are a few tips to keep in mind when sawing metal: Be sure to hold the saw lightly; do not grip the handle and force the saw. A sharp saw blade should do the job without being forced with a heavy hand. To decrease rough friction of the blade, use beeswax or Bur-Life on it prior to sawing. To turn a corner, turn the metal, not the saw frame. For a sharp corner, turn the metal and the saw at the same time while sawing.

SAWING TIPS

☐ If you're following a line, it can be helpful to cut between two lines instead of trying to stay on one. To do this, use a thin marker or scribe to draw or scribe a guideline a few millimeters on each side of your cutting line to help guide your eye and saw blade.

☐ Practice makes perfect! You'll go through a lot of blades, but don't worry. This happens to everyone until they get a natural feel for sawing.

WHAT YOU'LL NEED

Sheet metal to be sawed, any gauge
Saw frame and spare blades
Beeswax or Bur-Life blade lubricant

MOUNTING THE BLADE IN THE SAW FRAME

1 To attach the blade to the saw frame, hold the frame in one hand and the blade in the other. Be sure to have a solid surface available, such as your workbench, so that you can push the blade in tightly and be sure it's taut. The saw blade should be facing outward, its teeth pointing down toward the handle of the saw (A).

2 Place the blade into the grooves of the frame, and tighten the top thumb screw (B).

3 Push the handle of the saw against your workbench, and tighten the lower screw. The blade will be taut and should make a high pinging sound when plucked.

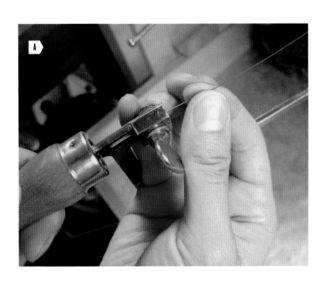

A

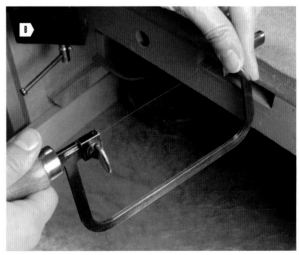

B

STARTING TO CUT

1 Hold your saw gently, and let the blade do the work. To begin cutting, place the workpiece on your bench pin, and hold your saw frame with its blade at the cutting point. Your other hand should be keeping the metal in place. Be careful to keep your fingers clear of the blade.

2 Your first cut should be on a slight 45° angle, with the top of the saw frame farther away from you. Place the saw blade against the metal about three-quarters of the way down the blade, and gently pull the saw downward. Gently move the saw up and down into the metal; the cutting occurs on each down stroke (A). After the first cut, bring the saw to a 90° angle from the metal (straight up and down, with the top edge of the saw frame perpendicular to your worktable), and continue to saw. When first learning to use a saw frame, breakage is very common. You will break a lot of saw blades in the beginning, but try not to get frustrated, and take your time.

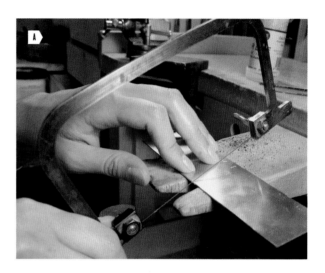

ORNAMENT NECKLACE BY JENNIFER CHIN,
14K gold

I made this necklace from tubing and wire, using a tube-cutting jig to cut the individual pieces. The tube cutter allowed me to get all the pieces at the exact same thickness. The many components were then soldered together.
PHOTO BY ALLEN BRYAN

DRILLING

Drilling is useful for creating holes in metal for functional and ornamental reasons. To properly drill holes in metal, you must create a guide divot in which the drill bit can sit as you begin drilling. This divot or shallow dent in the surface of the metal acts as a guide for the tip of the bit and keeps the bit from "dancing around" on the metal and creating surface scratches as the bit spins. To create a divot, use a small, pointed steel tool called a center punch, which when struck with a single blow from a hammer, creates a dent in the surface of the metal.

Drill bits are used with a jeweler's flexible shaft (or flex shaft), an invaluable tool that can be used for a variety of operations, including drilling, sanding, grinding, carving, polishing, and more. It's a rotary-style tool that consists of a motor, a long pliable shaft with a hand piece, and a foot pedal used to control the speed of the attached tool (similar to a sewing machine pedal). The motor should be mounted on a tall, swinging hook high enough to let you use the tool above and below a bench pin but also low enough to allow the hand piece to work at any angle. Drill bits, burrs, and texturizing attachments are inserted into the hand piece of the flex shaft with a chuck key and can be used for a variety of tasks. Keep a wide selection of burrs and drill bits on hand to make tasks easier and more convenient. When not in use, the shaft should be hung straight down from its hook, so as not to damage its internal components.

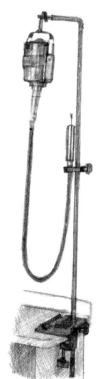

A flexible shaft on its swinging hook.

LOTUS CUFF BY CHIHIRO MAKIO, *sterling and gold-plated silver, glass beads*

This bracelet required many drilled holes along its edge. The glass beads were artfully woven through the holes, so the holes are functional as well as decorative.
PHOTO BY IVO M. VERMEULEN

DRILLING & PIERCING AN INTERIOR SHAPE

Some drilling projects may require you to cut out an interior shape in sheet metal. For that, you can use drilling to begin an entry hole for piercing out the shape. Drill a hole where the piercing will begin, and insert a saw blade through the drilled hole. You can then cut from the interior without starting the cut from the edge of the sheet.

WHAT YOU'LL NEED

Essential workbench tools (see page 22)
Sheet metal to be pierced, any gauge
Steel block
Wood block
Flexible shaft
Small drill bit
Saw frame and blades
Beeswax or Bur-Life

1 Determine where you need to drill your hole. Place your metal and steel block on your workbench. Place the tip of a center punch tool where your hole will be drilled, and tap it lightly with a chasing hammer to create a small indent (A). The indent will guide your drill bit. Without it, the drill is inclined to dance across the surface of your metal and scratch the surface.

2 Place the metal on your wood block. Secure the drill bit in the flexible shaft, and place the tip in the indent at a 90° angle to the metal (perpendicular to the metal). Drill the hole using an even, medium speed (B).

3 To begin sawing the metal, release the bottom end of the saw blade from its frame, and insert it through your drilled hole. Reattach the blade to the frame, and tighten the thumb screw. Be careful not to let your metal twist around, as it will break the saw blade easily. Saw out your interior shape (C), and then release the saw blade from the lower nut on the saw frame and slide your pierced metal off. Reattach the blade, and tighten the thumb screw.

FILING

After sawing or piercing, you'll often have to file your metal to remove burrs and even up rough edges. Hand, or "bastard," files are used as a first step to remove metal when finishing a piece. It's important to begin with a coarser file and work up to a fine file so that any marks made by the previous file are removed by the next. Files are graded from 00 to 8 (00 having the coarsest cut, 2 having a medium cut, and 4–8 having the finest). Needle files are smaller versions of hand files and are used for finer detail and finishing work.

Files come in many shapes, the most popular being flat, round, and half-round. Needle files are often sold in sets and come in round, square, barrette, triangle, and many more shapes. Riffler files are bent-needle files used to get into hard-to-reach places. Take good care of your files and they'll last for many years; keep them separated so that they don't rub against—and dull—one another, and use a soft brass brush to clean the teeth of your files.

Needle files in various shapes (from left to right): barrette, knife, round, equaling, and half-round.

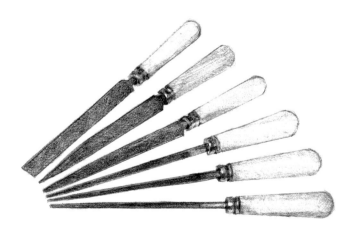

Hand files in various shapes (from top to bottom): flat, barrette, half-round, square, three square, and round.

This illustration shows the overall shape of each hand file.

USING A METAL FILE

When using files, it's important to take your time, keep your direction level, and only file in one forward-cutting movement. Avoid moving the file back and forth in a sawing motion, as this will dull the file's teeth. Be sure to pause and check your work often; it's impossible to replace lost metal when filing, so take care not to remove too much.

WHAT YOU'LL NEED

Essential workbench tools (see page 22)
Sheet metal to be filed, any gauge
Hand file of your choice

1 Rest the metal to be filed against the bench pin, or clamp it into a bench-top vise. Always use a stabilizing surface (such as a bench pin) to file against, for more controlled cutting strokes. With your index finger on top of the file, move the file with a firm, even stroke along the edge of the metal. Lift your file, and repeat the stroke.

Filing is made easier if you clamp your sheet metal in a bench vise.

SANDING & FINISHING

Sandpaper is an essential finishing material for removing excess solder, smoothing edges, and removing deep file marks. Abrasive paper for metal is different than wood sandpaper. It lasts longer and can be used wet or dry. Having sandpaper in many grits on hand is a good idea, but many jewelers generally use 220–600 grit papers, with 200 being the coarsest and 600 the finest. To achieve a smooth finish on metal, you begin with coarser grits and gradually sand with finer and finer grits. It's an important step to remove all traces of unintended filing marks. Lessons and projects in this book use 220-, 320-, and 400-grit papers.

Created from flat pieces of wood (approximately 1 x 10 inches) and strips of sandpaper, sanding sticks allow for handheld sanding operations. Wrap a strip of sandpaper around the wood and tape it to secure.

Green kitchen scrub pads (on the left in the image at left) and steel wool are excellent tools for achieving a matte brushed finish on metal. The pads, used wet or dry, texture the surface without removing any metal.

Metal brushes (on the right in the image at left) also make excellent tools to clean and burnish metal to a shiny finish. Brass brushes can be used wet with soap and water, while steel brushes should always be kept dry, as they will rust when exposed to moisture. Brass brushes can also be used dry but only with yellow metals, as these brushes can discolor the surface of metals such as sterling silver and white gold.

SANDING TIP

To achieve perfectly even sanding on a workpiece, lay your metal workpiece flat on sandpaper with the side you wish to sand face down. While gripping the metal in your fingers, move it in a figure-eight pattern to sand all the surfaces to an equal level.

Another useful sanding tool is the small split mandrel attachment for the flexible shaft. Cut long strips of sandpaper (¼-inch wide x length of the sandpaper piece) and wind them onto the mandrel. Use progressively finer grits to achieve a smooth surface and remove file marks.

BENDING & SHAPING

Bending metal wire and sheet is useful to form rings and bracelets or to otherwise alter metal into another shape. Be sure your metal is annealed, use forming tools (such as pliers, mandrels, and rawhide hammers), and shape the metal as desired.

MANDRELS

Mandrels are forms around which metal is wrapped and shaped. Commercial mandrels come in many shapes and sizes. They can be tapered, stepped, or have an even width. Other objects (such as pipes, tubing, and dowels) can be used for forming and wrapping. Most round ring mandrels have handy ring-size measurements, from sizes 1 through 16. Use these guides when forming rings to an exact size.

Here, a rawhide hammer is used to form metal around a ring mandrel to create a perfectly round shape—in this case, a ring band. For best results, the mandrel should be slowly rotated in one hand while the hammer is held in the other, delivering even hammer blows to all sides of the workpiece. This way, all sides of the metal receive the same amount of hammering to form an even shape.

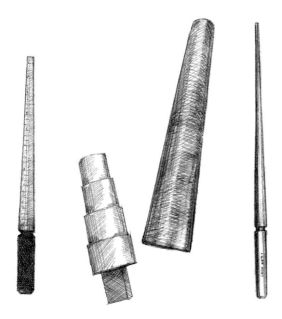

Shown from left to right are a ring mandrel, necklace and bracelet mandrels, and a bezel mandrel.

PLIERS

Flat-nose, round-nose, and needle-nose pliers are essential bench tools. They're great for holding, shaping, and forming. Be sure to buy several pairs that are comfortable in your hands, as you'll be using them often. Standard pliers come in many grades and sizes, and generally, a higher cost ensures better quality. Specialty pliers are also handy for specific operations but are not essential hand tools; examples include 90° pliers for creating perfect angles and beading and prong-closing pliers for stone setting.

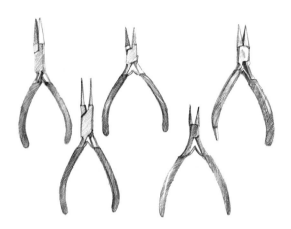

Various pliers (from left to right): long flat-nose, round-nose, flat-nose, bent chain-nose, and chain-nose.

HAMMERS AND MALLETS

Hammers are fundamental metalworking tools. While beginners only a need few, many metalsmiths' collections grow as their needs expand. Specialty hammers are used in forging, embossing, riveting, and many other processes. Choosing the right hammers depends on your workbench needs, but pictured below are two types I use on a regular basis.

Chasing hammers are the most commonly used and versatile hammers for jewelers. These multipurpose hammers are made from polished steel and have two-sided heads, one a ball-shaped side and the other a flat side. In addition to general hammering operations, they are used for the technique of chasing, which is a process of creating marks on the surface of metal that includes hammering texture and creating relief designs. They're weighted to give a firm but gentle blow, making them an excellent go-to hammer.

Mallets are used to shape metal without stretching or marring its surface. They have wide cylinder-shaped heads with flat faces. Rawhide, plastic, wood, and rubber are a few of the more popular hammer materials. Use a rawhide mallet (shown here) to hammer metal around a mandrel to create ring bands, bangle bracelets, or any round shape.

CUFF BRACELET BY LAURA PRESHONG, *sterling silver and blown glass*

This cuff bracelet was created by forming and hammering the metal around an oval mandrel with a rawhide hammer. **PHOTO BY ALLEN BRYAN**

MAKING JUMP RINGS

Creating your own findings (mechanisms such as earring wires, jump rings, and basic clasps) is a useful and money-saving venture. Jump rings are some of the most commonly used findings in jewelry making, either as connecting mechanisms or stand-alone components. I always keep many sizes on hand. You can purchase a handy tool called a jump ringer through jewelry supply retailers. This tool has a swiveling handle and an adjustable holder for mandrels; wires can be wrapped quickly around a mandrel with a turn of the handle.

WHAT YOU'LL NEED

Essential workbench tools (see page 22)

Annealed round wire, any metal and gauge

Saw frame

Round mandrel in the width of desired jump rings: Use the handle of a dapping tool, a thick nail, wooden dowel, or the like

1. Begin by wrapping the wire tightly and evenly around the mandrel, making sure each consecutive wrap touches the one before it.

2. After making the desired amount of rings, remove the wrapped wire from the mandrel, and hold the coil firmly on the bench pin. Hold your saw frame perpendicular to the coil, as pictured, and begin sawing through one side of the rings.

3. Saw all the way down, through all the rings, holding the saw at an angle. Hold the sawed jump rings tightly or set them aside as they're cut. Note that thicker-gauge jump rings may have a burr at the opening, so clean up as needed using a round needle file or sandpaper.

4. To open and close jump rings without marring their shape, hold each side with a pair of flat-nose pliers, and pull outward in an east/west direction (i.e., to the sides).

STERLING SILVER BRACELETS BY DONNA VEVERKA

These bracelets use jump rings as both a functional and decorative element: They act as links and clasp the ends, and they also create an interesting pattern. **PHOTO BY JAMES HULL**

MAKING FRENCH EARRING WIRES

Used often for dangling earring styles, French earring wires have a curved wire resembling a fish hook that passes through the earlobe on one end and holds an ornament with a loop on the other. A very common jewelry mechanism, French wires are simple to make and very attractive with many earring styles.

WHAT YOU'LL NEED

Essential workbench tools (see page 22)
Annealed sterling silver round wire, 22 gauge
Round-nose pliers

EVERGREEN EARRINGS BY JENNIFER CHIN, *sterling and fine silver*
These earrings have basic French wires. The open loop has been soldered shut due to the weight and design of the earrings.
PHOTO BY ALLEN BRYAN

1 Using flush cutters, cut a length of wire approximately 2½ inches long. File one end flat with a flat needle file, and file the other end to a rounded point.

2 Using a pair of round-nose pliers, bend the flat end of the wire into a loop around the narrow tip of the pliers. Be sure the loop is as closed as possible; the earring's ornament will hang from this.

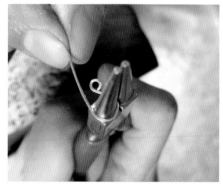

3 Bend the wire around the thicker section of the round pliers to make the U-shaped hook. This is the segment of wire that passes through the earlobe.

RIVETING

Rivets are excellent *cold-connection mechanisms* for connecting parts *without* using a soldered joint. Made with wire or tubing, rivets are an ancient mechanism used often in jewelry making. They can be made in any size, be decorative or hidden, and be used to bond practically any material. The following two lessons show the two most common riveting techniques.

A riveting hammer is a small hammer with a head that has one flat end and one chiseled end. The flat end is for flattening rivets and the chiseled for flaring rivets.

▷ Always create a starting depression in the metal with a center punch before drilling, otherwise the drill bit will dance across the surface of the metal without a guide.

▷ Use a flaring tool (a small, tapered hand tool) to flare the ends of tubing. Use a small dapping tool to flare, or make your own tool by filing a large nail or a burr into a tapered point.

▷ If your rivet bends during the hammering step, it's probably too long. Remove it and file it down to a smaller size.

▷ Flip the piece over and hammer the rivet equally on both sides. The ends need to be evenly flared for the rivet to be a good one.

▷ If a rivet needs to be placed in a hard-to-reach spot, preflare one end of the rivet before threading it through the sheet metal.

Various rivets (from left to right): brass split-tube rivet, nail-head rivet, tube rivet, silver split-tube rivet, hammered copper rivet.

MAKING A WIRE RIVET

A rivet consists of a metal pin (wire) inserted through a hole in parts to be joined. The protruding tips on each end of the pin are flared and hammered to create a "mushroomed" head, securing the parts together. Wire rivets have many functional and decorative uses including joining parts that cannot be soldered (for example, riveting metal to wood or plastic) or adding ornamentation to a surface.

WHAT YOU'LL NEED

Essential workbench tools (see page 22)

Sheet metal, any gauge

Steel block

Center punch

Chasing or riveting hammer

Wood block

Drill bit of corresponding size to wire

Saw frame

Round wire, any gauge

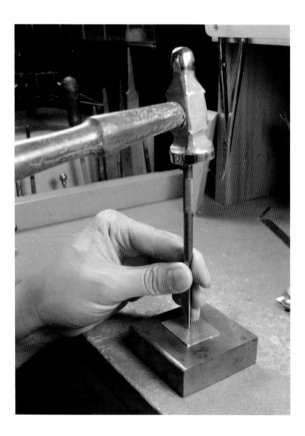

❶ Place the sheet metal on the steel block, and using a center punch and hammer, tap a depression into the sheet metal where the rivet will be located.

❷ Remove the steel block and replace with a wood block. Drill a hole at the depression using a drill bit of corresponding size to the round riveting wire. Be sure to drill on a wooden surface, as drilling on a metal surface won't allow a bit to fully drill through your workpiece and can damage the drill bit.

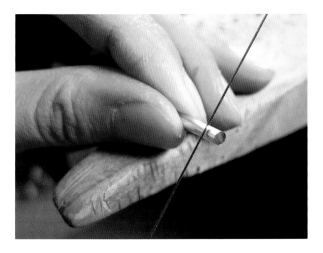

3 Using your saw, cut a segment of rivet wire measuring approximately 2mm longer than the thickness of the sheet metal. Remove all burrs from the wire using a flat needle file.

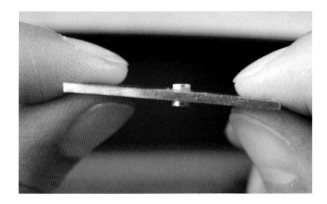

4 Push the wire through the hole in the sheet metal, and make sure an equal amount of wire is protruding from each side.

5 Place the metal onto a steel block. Hammer the wire facing you lightly a few times with the ball end of a chasing hammer or the chiseled end of a riveting hammer until it flares slightly. Hammering the wire with either of these hammers will mushroom the metal outward, making it wider than the hole in which it sits.

6 Flip the sheet metal over, check again that there's an equal amount of wire on each side, hammer the wire lightly again with the same end of your hammer, and flip over again. Repeat until the wire is flattened and stretched. Use the flat end of the chasing or riveting hammer to smooth the surface of the rivet.

MAKING A TUBE RIVET

A tube rivet is the same as a wire rivet, except that it uses a segment of tubing instead of wire for the joining pin. Tubing is a hollow rod. Rivets created from tubing are excellent for functional purposes, such as grommets and threading holes. Tube rivets can also be flared and embellished as decorative elements in design.

To create a rivet using tubing, begin by following steps 1 and 2 in the previous lesson, and make sure to use a drill bit of corresponding size to the width of the tubing.

WHAT YOU'LL NEED

Essential workbench tools (see page 22)

Sheet metal, any gauge

Steel block

Center punch

Chasing hammer

Drill bit of corresponding size to tubing

Wood block

Tubing, no smaller than 3mm

Flaring tool

1 After completing steps 1 and 2 from the previous lesson, start by cutting a length of round tubing with your jeweler's saw that is approximately 3mm longer than the thickness of the sheet metal. Use a small steel ruler to measure accurately. After cutting, file the tubing with a flat needle file to remove burrs.

2 Push the tubing through the drilled hole in the sheet metal, and place onto the steel block.

3 Insert a flaring tool (a small, tapered hand tool) into the tubing, and lightly tap once with the chasing hammer (A).

4 Flip the sheet over, and check that the tubing is even on both sides. Repeat with the flaring tool, tapping only once.

5 Continue to flip and tap, adjusting the tubing as needed until it is tight and even.

6 Using the ball end of the chasing hammer, continue to flare and flatten the tube (without the flaring tool) until it is a flat donut shape on both sides (B).

DOUBLE OVAL NECKLACE BY LISA CROWDER, *sterling silver*

This necklace uses tube rivets to connect the elements in the piece. **PHOTO BY HAP SAKWA**

DECORATIVE RIVET IDEAS

Rivets are excellent for connecting elements that cannot be soldered as well as for use as a decorative feature. These pieces show how rivets work both as fasteners and design details.

COCOON TEMPLE RING BY LISA CROWDER, *sterling silver*

This ring uses a decorative and also functional rivet to close its band and attach its top elements. The rivet has an elongated ball on one side and has been hammered flat on the inner side of the ring band to secure it. **PHOTO BY HAP SAKWA**

BUTTERCUP EARRINGS BY LAUREN SCHLOSSBERG, *sterling silver and enamel*

These earrings use small tube rivets to attach the flower elements. They work decoratively in the piece as the center of the flowers and also functionally as connecting mechanisms. **PHOTO BY HAP SAKWA**

BASIC SOLDERING OVERVIEW

Joining metal components together as one is called *soldering* or *brazing*. After preliminary fabrication, annealing, and shaping, soldering is usually the next step. The basic steps are outlined opposite, but before beginning, keep a few things in mind: Preparation is key to successful soldering. Be sure to have the right amount of solder and other stabilizing elements on hand, such as binding wire and locking tweezers, to ensure that your workpiece doesn't move while soldering.

With multiple soldering jobs, the different grades of solder come in handy. Always use hard solder for your first joint, follow with medium, and then easy (see page 52 for more on the grades). If your object requires more than three soldering operations, be very careful around previous joints, and use easy or medium solders.

During final finishing stages of sanding and/or polishing, metal can sometimes reveal discoloration on its surface, which is called *firescale*. Firescale usually shows up as a purple or copper stain in the metal and forms whenever silver or gold containing copper is heated above 1000°F (537°C). (See page 58 for information about firescale removal.)

Intuitive response to each unique soldering job will come with practice. Try not to get frustrated; the key is to remain positive and keep working. Think of soldering as you would an exercise in driving: Every situation is new, with different reactions needed to get where you're going. Soldering and directing heat will become second nature with practice.

NECKLACE BY PETRA SEIBERTOVA, *sterling silver and tourmalinated quartz*

This necklace was created using wire. After the ends of the wires were balled using a torch, the wires were soldered together at various points to join them and also around the bezel holding the stone. **PHOTO BY ADAM KRAUTH**

1. Be sure that your metal is clean, because the solder won't flow if your workpiece is dirty. Clean your metal with a soapy, wet green scrub pad or a brass brush, or by immersing it in a hot pickle solution (see page 57 for more on pickle). Being prepared will make a huge difference during a soldering job, and you'll be able to solder more successfully with less cleanup and fewer meltdowns.

2. The properly prepared components must then be "fluxed" at the joints you wish to make. With a small paintbrush, apply flux to joints you wish to solder together (see page 52).

3. Using flush cutters or shears, cut solder as needed. The amount of solder depends on the size of the seam to be closed. If the seam has been properly prepared and meets perfectly, only a small amount of solder is needed. Too much solder turns into more cleanup later on, so use it sparingly for a neater joint.

4. At this point, turn on your torch (see page 20), and heat your workpiece on a fireproof surface, being sure to keep even heat on the entire object. The flux will bubble, boil, and become glassy; this is your cue that the metal is hot enough to solder.

5. Working quickly, place a small ball of solder onto the seam while continuing to heat the object. The solder will then flow into the joint. Be careful not to overheat your metal—stop as soon as the solder has flowed. Turn off your torch to allow your workpiece to cool for about a minute, and then place it into warm pickle solution using copper tongs (see page 57). After your metal is clean, remove it from the pickle, and rinse it in cold water. Clean silver will be bright white; copper and brass will be pink. Further fabrication processes and soldering follow as needed.

GIZMO BRACELETS BY JENNIFER CHIN, *sterling silver*

These bracelets required many soldering operations, as they are made up of individually cut segments of tubing and wire connected together to form solid bangle bracelets. **PHOTO BY ALLEN BRYAN**

SOLDER & FLUX

Solders are alloys of precious metals that have lower melting points than the metals they're intended to connect. The connection is created when solder is heated to its flowing point before the primary metals can melt. After considering the various solders here, we'll move on to the different soldering methods (see page 55).

Silver solder contains zinc, which controls its melting range. The amount of zinc results in five different grades of solder with different flowing temperatures, enabling jewelers to execute repeated solderings on a single piece. Silver solder is used to join sterling silver, copper, and brass throughout this book.

The various karats of gold solders are similar to silver solder, except that they're an alloy of gold and silver with cadmium added to lower the melting point. Gold solder is expensive and mostly used to solder with gold.

Silver and gold solders in all grades are available in several forms, such as wire, sheet, and paste. Choosing one form over another depends on your habits and needs. I most often use wire solder, which is easier to cut than sheet solder and is often used for pick or wire soldering. Sheet solder is excellent when you're placing solder onto joints before applying heat, as its flat shape will keep the solder chips in place while flux bubbles away.

SOLDER MELTING POINTS & USES

The harder the solder, the higher its melting point. Because of this, a piece can be soldered multiple times using solders with different melting points. Always start with hard solder, follow with medium solder, and then use easy solder for the last soldering operation, so as not to flow the previously soldered joints.

EXTRAHARD SOLDER (IT SOLDER)

Has a melting point of 1370°F (743°C) and contains the highest amount of silver (75%), making it the highest-temperature solder. This solder isn't used for any of the projects in this book.

HARD SOLDER

Has a melting point of 1365°F (741°C) and is typically used for the first seam on a piece if there will be more than one solder joint. It's possible to use hard solder more than once with careful heat monitoring and timing.

MEDIUM SOLDER

Has a melting point of 1275°F (691°C) and should be used after hard soldering. It can sometimes be "sticky" and not flow properly.

EASY SOLDER

Has a melting point of 1240°F (682°C) and is used for soldering findings, attachments, and jump rings. It's a good-flowing solder typically used for a final seam.

EXTRA-EASY SOLDER

Has a melting point of 1145°F (618°C). It should be used as a last resort, as it tends to have a yellowish color. Use it when easy solder has already been used on a workpiece.

Wire and sheet solder cut into chips. Sheet solders cut into 1mm chips are good for soldering small bezel wires, jump rings, and earring posts.

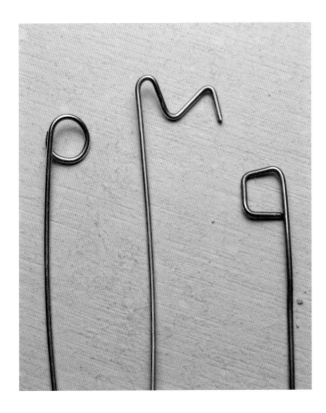

To identify the different melting points of wire solders, it's helpful to bend a shape into one end. Using metal pliers, jewelers bend these symbols on one end of each type of wire (from left to right): easy, medium, and hard.

SILVER SOLDER
MELTING & FLOW TEMPERATURES

As mentioned previously, solder is a metal filler material used to join two metals together. When heated, solder will melt faster than metal, due to the low-temperature alloys in its composition. In other words, the metal has a higher melting point than the solder. The term *melting point* refers to the temperature at which metal is no longer solid. During the soldering process, the *flowing point* of the metal occurs when metal becomes liquid and is drawing into a joint by capillary action.

SOLDER TYPE	MELTING POINT	FLOWING POINT
IT	1370°F (743°C)	1490°F (810°C)
HARD	1365°F (741°C)	1450°F (788°C)
MEDIUM	1275°F (691°C)	1360°F (738°C)
EASY	1240°F (682°C)	1325°F (718°C)
EXTRA-EASY	1145°F (618°C)	1207°F (653°C)

The amount of solder used varies depending on the size of the joint to be soldered. When preparing your solder, it's important to consider the size of the area you need to fill with solder. If the metals meet properly with no space between them, very little solder will be needed to fill the joint. A 1mm chip or square of solder is more than enough to close a thin bezel or solder a post or jump ring to an earring. A ring band has a thicker wall than a bezel, requiring more solder to make up for the surface area within the joint. Consider the gauge of your metal and how much metal would be needed to fill the thin space within a joint. Solder doesn't behave like glue: It will not fill large gaps even if a lot is used; it will more likely flow around the joint, making cleanup much more tedious. Less is more when soldering; the right amount to use for different tasks will become clear with time and practice.

Flux is a chemical used to prevent oxidation during soldering or heating. Applied before any heating or soldering begins, the flux absorbs oxygen before it has a chance to make an oxide (tarnished) layer that hinders soldering. Jewelry fluxes come in many forms, from fluoride-based liquids to borax-based pastes. Different types of flux are effective at various heat levels, most commonly between 1100°F (593°C) and 1500°F (815°C). I use a paste flux throughout the book during all soldering operations.

Applied with a small paintbrush, paste flux has a thick, sticky texture that allows for easy application on soldering areas.

SOLDERING TOOLS

Below are a few of the most commonly used soldering tools. These essential tools are used during heating and joining operations to place solder and adjust elements as they're being heated—and they also can be used to protect an area from overheating during these processes. The downside to some of these aids is that they often rob heat from your workpiece. Locking tweezers and binding wire, for example, can act as a "heat sink," absorbing heat and prolonging a soldering job.

SOLDERING PICKS

Use these to pick up solder for placement on a workpiece. They're usually made of titanium, which will stay cool during heating.

TWEEZERS

Tweezers are essential for picking up metals and adjusting placement of components. In addition to regular tweezers, you should have a few locking pairs with insulated handles on hand. Locking tweezers are integral when soldering small parts to heavier components; for example, soldering a jump ring to a bezel requires locking tweezers not only to hold the ring but also to keep it from melting during the heating of the larger piece.

COPPER TONGS

Use these to place metal into, and retrieve it from, the pickle solution. Never put steel tools or wire in your pickle (see page 57 for more on this).

STRIKER

A striker is a tool used for igniting the torch flame. It creates a spark with a flint rubbing against a coarse steel surface.

THIRD HAND

A third hand holds locking tweezers in place and is useful for situations in which elements need temporary support during soldering.

STEEL BINDING WIRE

Flexible steel binding wire is useful for holding components together while they're being soldered.

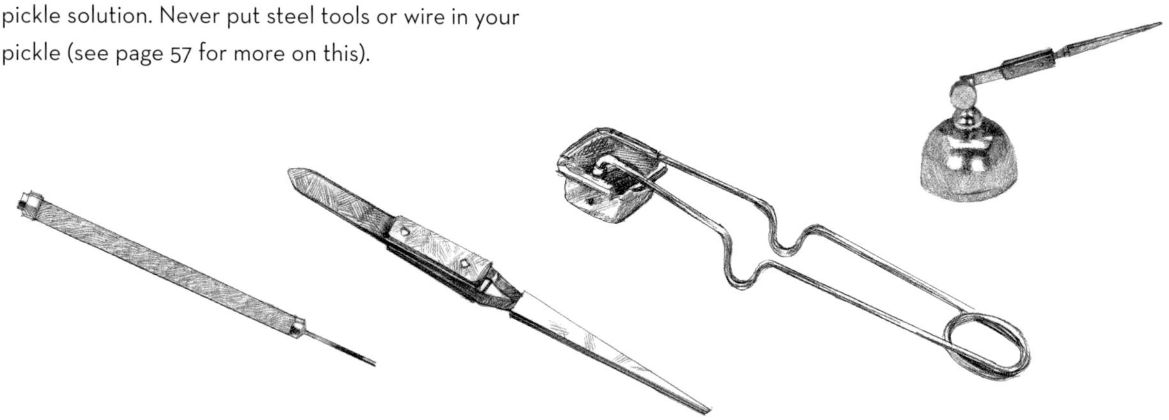

Shown above: a solder pick, locking tweezers, a torch striker, and a third hand.

SOLDERING METHODS

There are many ways to solder; no one technique is better than another. Each can be useful, depending on the job at hand. Here are a few common soldering techniques to use during different situations.

CHIP (PALLION) SOLDERING

This form of soldering uses small chips of solder to fill a joint. Solder in sheet form is cut into strips, which are then cut into tiny squares—or chips, or pallions (see photo on page 52)—that are placed directly onto a fluxed solder seam before heating. This allows for quick and controlled soldering, as the solder is already in place before the heating begins. The disadvantage is the tedious cutting and placement of the chips and the probable necessity of repositioning after the flux boils. I use this method when placing many chips of solder on a workpiece; the chips are placed where I need them to be and then heated and flowed. Use this method for the cabochon brooch project (page 120) when soldering the decorative silver balls to the points of the star.

WIRE (STICK) SOLDERING

Wire soldering is an efficient, less-tedious method of soldering but takes a more experienced and steady hand. In this method, a length of wire solder is grasped with locking tweezers and touched down on the joint at exactly the moment when the metal is ready. If the metal isn't hot enough, the solder will blob into a mess. A light touch is needed to fill a joint without overflowing it. Use this method in the retro bracelet project (page 82) to solder the seams of the rings using hard solder held in tweezers.

Before the torch is lit, the joint to be soldered is painted with flux paste and chips of solder are placed at the joint.

The joint of a ring band is soldered shut here using a length of hard wire solder held with locking tweezers. The joint was fluxed and heated, and the wire solder is touching down at the joint.

PICK SOLDERING

Pick soldering is a method that mixes the conveniences of both chip and wire soldering. Precut pieces are placed on a fireproof soldering board and are then heated into balls and picked up with a soldering pick. When a workpiece is ready, the solder is placed into the seam to be joined using the pick. This is a good method to use for repetitive work or if the solder placement on a workpiece is complicated. Use this method in the forged chain necklace project (page 80) to solder shut the jump rings.

SWEAT SOLDERING (TINNING)

Sweat soldering is a method that utilizes either wire or sheet solder and is commonly used when soldering metal sheets, or components with large surface areas, together. Solder is flowed onto the surface of a metal workpiece, cooled, and then refluxed with a secondary overlay piece on top. The advantage is that the solder has already flowed where you want it to be (chips of solder can often jump around while flux boils and can flow out of control into unintended areas); and it provides more control when soldering large and small pieces together. Use this method for the lamination inlay lesson (page 142). Preflow solder onto components, lay them solder side down on the fluxed metal to be connected, and heat the entire piece to flow the solder.

In pick soldering, precut pieces of wire solder and a soldering pick are used. When heat is applied, the pieces of solder melt into balls and can be picked up with the tip of a steel pick and then placed onto a seam.

For the sweat soldering pictured here, the solder is preflowed onto round disks that are then joined to a sheet. The two disks on the worktable have solder flowed onto them. The disks on the sheet have been placed solder side down. When heated, the disks will solder to the sheet.

GALAXY PIN BY CHIHIRO MAKIO, *sterling silver*

This pin was created with components that were sweat soldered to sheet metal. Preflowed solder was flowed onto the back sides of the curled wire, and beads were placed as desired. The metals were then heated until the solder flowed again. **PHOTO BY IVO M. VERMEULEN**

PICKLE

Pickling is the chemical cleaning of metal after heating or soldering. Pickle can be purchased through jeweler's supply companies (see Resources) and comes in a dry, powdered form. Mixed with water, it makes a strong acid bath that dissolves surface oxidation and flux residue. Pickle mixtures should be kept in a dedicated heating container (a Crock-Pot with a lid) for best results. Pickle is most effective when hot; keep the Crock-Pot at the Warm setting for an effective cleaning temperature. Cold pickle will remove surface residue but will take much longer to clean the metal. Be sure to read any instructions provided with purchased pickle and take care when handling it.

After soldering, allow your workpiece to cool slightly, or quench it in water, and then place it into the pickle until it's clean. Silver will have a bright white finish after heating and pickling. Always use copper tongs with pickle. (Pickle can become contaminated by steel entering the pickle pot. If the pickle has been used to clean sterling silver, copper ions will latch onto the water in the pickle. Steel entering the acid will act as a catalyst for releasing the copper ions. These ions will attach themselves to metal pieces in the pot and will copper-plate the metal.) Rinse your workpiece in cold water or in a solution of water and baking soda to neutralize any remaining acid (1 teaspoon of baking soda per cup of water).

Clean silver will appear white as the workpiece is removed from the pickle pot.

It's very important to protect yourself while mixing or using pickle solutions. Wearing safety goggles, rubber gloves, and an apron will help prevent injury from splashes. Keeping a box of baking soda close at hand is a good remedy to neutralize spills. A nontoxic version of pickle can be made with vinegar and salt; use 1 tablespoon of salt for every cup of vinegar, mix them together in a Crock-Pot, and keep the pot on the Warm setting.

Pickle will eventually become spent and need to be changed. This will become evident when it turns greenish-blue and cleans metal very slowly. To dispose of pickle, put your pickle pot into a sink, and add half a cup of baking soda to neutralize the acid. The pickle will bubble and foam; sprinkle in several more tablespoons of baking soda until the foaming subsides. Add water, and pour the neutral acid down a sink drain or into a toilet.

FIRESCALE

The appearance of firescale is a common occurrence when soldering. Firescale is an oxide of copper that occurs in sterling silver and gold alloys and appears as a purple stain on the surface of the metal when that metal has been heated for too long or after many soldering operations. Firescale appears during finishing processes (sanding and polishing) after top layers of fine silver are removed. You can remove firescale on sterling silver or gold by sanding away the discoloration.

Another technique to remove firescale on sterling silver is building up a layer of fine silver over the surface, a process called *depletion gilding*. This thin top layer of fine silver covers the firescale and is useful for pieces with intricate surface detail that may be difficult to sand. To do this, carefully heat the piece just until the silver starts to turn red (approximately 900°F/482°C), allow to cool for a few minutes, and then place it into the pickle. After a few minutes in the pickle, remove the piece and brush it with a brass brush under running water. Repeat this 6–8 times.

Used to keep pickle warm, a ceramic Crock-Pot with a lid is perfect for cleaning oxidation and flux residue on metal.

Always use copper tongs with pickle; avoid using any steel tools for the pickling process.

LESSON 9 — SOLDERING A SEAM

In this lesson, we use the torch to solder for the first time. This lesson shows how to solder the seam on a sterling silver ring band that has been fabricated and formed into a round ring shape. You can use any precious or base metals for this lesson, wire or sheet and so on. The goal is to work with solder for the first time and observe how it is heated and flows into a seam, making a connection.

WHAT YOU'LL NEED

Basic soldering tool kit (see page 23)
Metal to be joined (sterling silver is used here)
Hard silver sheet or wire solder

1 Begin by painting a thin layer of flux paste on your workpiece seam (A).

2 Snip small strips or chips of hard solder, and lay them to the side on your soldering surface. Be sure not to mix types of solder; keep them properly identified.

3 Light your torch and adjust to a bushy, pulsing flame, deep blue in color.

4 With your torch in one hand and your solder pick in the other, heat your solder chip until it balls, and then pick up with your solder pick (B).

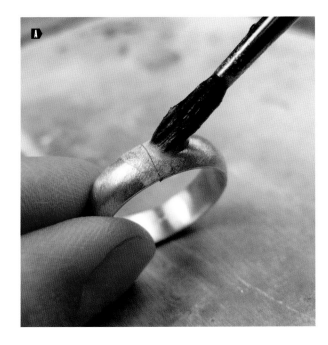

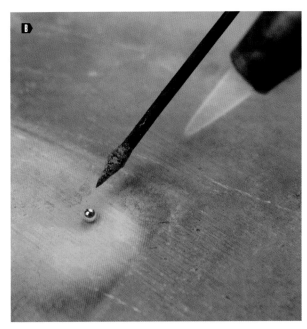

5 Heat the entire piece gently with a soft flame. The flux will turn a chalky white as the water evaporates. It will bubble and finally turn into a clear fluid; this is the cue that the metal is hot enough for soldering.

6 When the flux is glassy, carefully place the solder ball on your seam. Be sure it's exactly over the seam, or your solder can jump away from the joint (C).

Alternately, you can place your solder chip on your seam before heating. The chip will dance around as the flux is heated, so use the tip of your solder pick to reposition the solder.

7 Keep your torch moving, working in concentric circles and concentrating the flame around the seam.

8 Your solder ball will become shiny and flow neatly into the joint. Stop heating immediately once the solder has completely flowed into the seam (D).

9 Allow your piece to cool slightly, and use copper tongs to quench it in the hot pickle solution. Keep your workpiece in the pickle until it is clean and white (5–10 minutes), and then rinse in water.

TIPS FOR SUCCESSFUL SOLDERING

SEAMS
Pieces to be soldered together must meet snugly. File or sand components until there is no space between seams.

CLEAN PARTS
Components must be clean. Use a brass brush or a green scrub pad wet with some dish soap to remove dirt and grease before soldering.

FLUX
Flux keeps the metal clean so that solder will flow.

CONTINUOUS HEAT
Heat the entire piece continuously, directing your flame in circular movements around a joint. Solder will flow toward heat, so heat around where you want the solder to flow. Avoid concentrating your flame at the joint; let the heat travel through the entire piece.

METAL THICKNESS
Take into account the thickness of metals being joined. If you're soldering a small piece to a large one, the large piece will need more heat. It's important to always regulate temperature in each element so that they reach temperature at the same time. Heat the entire object evenly and keep your torch moving to maintain the same temperature throughout the piece. If one piece doesn't reach the necessary temperature, the solder won't flow properly.

OBSERVATION
Don't overheat. Prolonging the process can result in damage to your workpiece. You can always clean and reflux if your solder joint is stubborn. Know when to back off (this will come with practice).

LIGHTING
Temperature is read through color changes in the metal that are best seen in dim light. Shield your soldering bench from bright light.

SOLDERING TROUBLESHOOTING

PROBLEM	POSSIBLE CAUSE(S)
The solder didn't flow.	The solder or metal was dirty. Not enough flux or no flux. Torch flame was too low.
Solder flowed but not in the seam.	The piece wasn't heated entirely. The seam didn't meet properly.
Broken joint (after solderiing).	The joint was moved before the solder hardened. The heating ended too early, and the solder flowed but not enough.
Meltdown	Too much heat, and flame sat in one spot for too long.

BAUHAUS BRACELET BY HILARY HACHEY, *sterling silver*

This bracelet was created from tubing and flat wire. The many elements were connected together by soldering with hard, medium, and easy solders. **PHOTO BY HAP SAKWA**

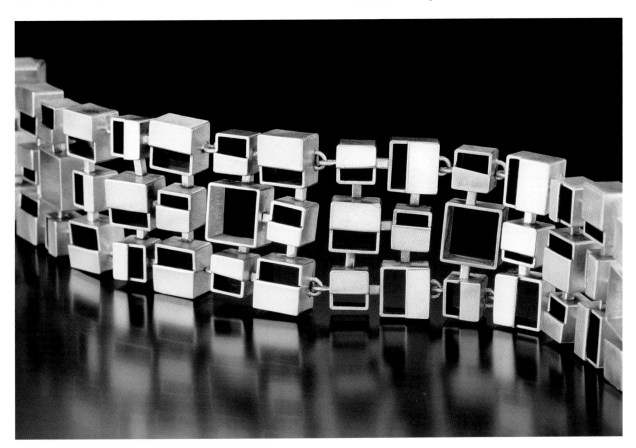

PROJECT
RIVETED COLLAR RING

This project uses the basic techniques of annealing, bending, and riveting. The simple ring can be embellished in many ways. Texture can be added to the sheet before forming, and the rivet can be more decorative if desired. I use 6 x 2mm rectangular wire here, but sheet or flat wire of any gauge can be used.

WHAT YOU'LL NEED

Essential workbench tools (see page 22)

Annealed sterling silver sheet or flat wire, any gauge

Ring mandrel

Chasing hammer

Tubing or wire to rivet

1 Cut your annealed sheet or flat wire to the desired width. The length will depend on the size needed (see ring-sizing guide on page 155). Cut the metal 6mm longer than the size needed, to accommodate the rivets.

2 Remove any saw marks from all edges with a needle file, and round the ends of the metal into slight curves (A).

3 Position the metal on your wood block, and drill one hole about 3mm in from the edge on each end of the metal using a bit size that corresponds to the width of the rivet material (B).

4 Bend the metal piece around a ring mandrel until it overlaps and the drilled holes line up (C). Tap lightly with a rawhide hammer; you want to retain the shape but not dent the overlapping end with the other end below it.

5 To create the rivet, cut the tubing or wire to approximately 3mm longer than the thickness of the two overlapping ring ends. File any burrs.

The finished ring from this project is on the left. The other rings pictured also contain rivets with tubing and wire. The ring in the center features a screw-head rivet created with 14K gold that is flared on the inside of the ring and holds the piece together. It is both decorative and functional. **PHOTO BY ALLEN BRYAN**

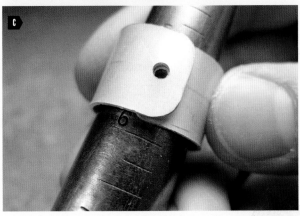

6 As one side of the rivet will be unreachable inside the band, you'll have to preflare it slightly. If using tubing to rivet, preflare one side slightly (D), and insert the tube into the holes from the inside, flared side on the inside of the band. If using wire to rivet, insert it into the holes while the ring is on the mandrel, and preflare the end of the rivet that's facing you. The mandrel will provide a metal surface against which to hammer. After the rivet mushrooms slightly, remove it and reinsert it from the inside of the band with the widened side now on the inside.

7 With the ring on the mandrel, flare the outer side of the rivet, and hammer with a chasing hammer until it is flat (E). The inner rivet will be flattened by the force of the hammer against the mandrel. Be careful about where your chasing hammer meets the metal, as unintentional marks on the ring band can be hard to remove.

8 Reshape the ring with the rawhide mallet. Sand inside and out, making sure the inner rivet will be smooth when worn.

9 Finish the surface by rubbing with a green scrub pad.

PROJECT
RIBBON EARRINGS

As with the previous project, making these earrings involves annealing, bending, and soldering. These earrings can be a starting point for using many other techniques. You can add hammered texture to the edges, surface detail, or oxidation to embellish this design. Play with length and ribbon shape to create your own one-of-a-kind earrings.

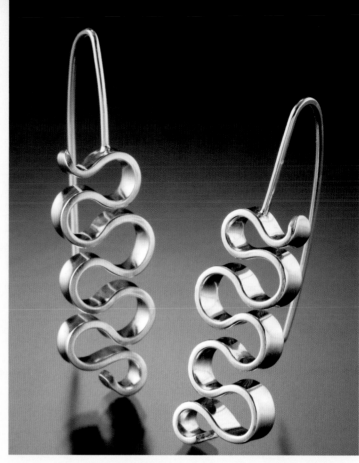

These ribbon earrings, created from sheet metal, combine the fabrication techniques of sawing, filing, annealing, and forming jump rings with soldering.
PHOTO BY ALLEN BRYAN

WHAT YOU'LL NEED

Essential workbench tools (see page 22)

Basic soldering tool kit (see page 23)

Sterling silver sheet, 20–22 gauge

2 pairs of round pliers

Bezel mandrel

Sterling silver round wire, 20 gauge

Hard solder

Half-round pliers

Rawhide mallet

❶ Measure and saw out two segments of sheet metal, each measuring 4 inches x 4mm.

❷ File and round the edges of your segments so that there are no sharp edges (A). Sand with 400-grit sandpaper, removing all file marks.

❸ Anneal the metal and quench.

❹ Using round pliers, begin curling one of the metal strips into a loop on one end (B). Holding the metal just above the first loop, bend the wire again. Continue until you've formed the metal into approximately three even S shapes (C). Curl the end as desired, and repeat the process with the other strip.

    Shape these ribbons into a tighter or looser shape, according to your preference. Use two pairs of round pliers or a round bezel mandrel to help shape the ribbons.

64

ESSENTIAL FABRICATION & SOLDERING TECHNIQUES

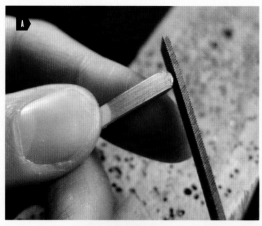

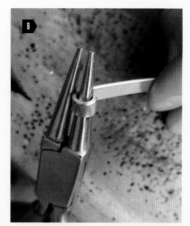

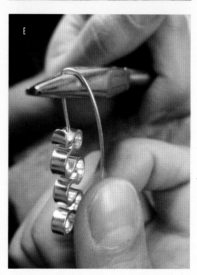

5 Cut two segments of wire approximately 2 inches each. File each so that one end is flat and the other is rounded.

6 Solder the wire to the top of each ribbon shape using hard solder (D), and then pickle and dry the earrings.

7 Using half-round pliers, grasp the wire ½-inch from the earring, and bend the wire, adding a slight curve to the rest of the wire with your round pliers (E).

8 The wire will be soft after soldering. Hammer it lightly or burnish with round pliers to work-harden the wire until it is stiff and resilient.

9 Finish with a steel brush.

FIZZY PENDANT

This is a more intermediate soldering project that uses commercially made tubing. (Note that the tube diameter listings refer to outside diameters (from outer edge to outer edge). It has many soldering joints that require an attention to detail and a quick hand, but it's a great piece for practicing your soldering skills. Take your time, make sure you execute the first steps well, and the rest will come easily. In the end, you'll have a beautiful and delicate work of art you can be proud to wear.

The piece shown here was constructed using the methods outlined in the project steps, but the tubing diameters are slightly different from those in the instructions. This results in a slight difference in the spacing between the concentric rings, but the overall effect is comparable. **PHOTO BY ALLEN BRYAN**

WHAT YOU'LL NEED

Essential workbench tools (see page 22)

Basic soldering tool kit (see page 23)

Round tubing in diameters of 8mm, 6mm, 4mm, and 2mm

Round sterling wire, 18 gauge

Hard, medium, and easy solders

1 Begin by cutting the tubing into approximately 4mm lengths. Use a tube cutter to create evenly sized segments. Cut seven pieces each of the 8mm, 6mm, and 4mm tubing and six pieces of the 2mm tubing.

2 With a round needle file, remove any burrs on the insides and outsides of the tubing created from sawing. Sand the faces (the sides) on 320-grit sandpaper to remove saw marks.

3 Lay all the pieces out on a soldering surface. Be sure the surface is very flat to ensure the tubes are soldered evenly.

4 Create seven concentric circles of the 4mm, 6mm, and 8mm tubing by placing the 4mm and 6mm segments one inside the other within the 8mm segments (A).

5 Flux the tubes at the points where they all meet, and cut seven 3mm snips of hard solder. Cutting a little extra solder is a good idea in case the chips are misplaced or flow into the wrong spot.

6 Solder the tubes together, placing a ball of solder where the three edges of the tubing meet, and heat until it flows (B). The solder should flow into the spaces between each tube all the way through. Be careful not to linger too long with your flame on the tubing, as it will melt easily. Pickle the segments.

7 After the seven groupings are clean and dry, sand the faces (both sides) of each with 220-grit sandpaper until the joint where the three tubes meet appears clean and continuous.

8 Lay the segments together on the soldering board, one in the center with the other six surrounding it, making sure all pieces are touching and in a tight pattern. Flux all joints in between the individual segments.

9 Cut small snips of medium solder (1mm–2mm), and light your torch. Heat the pendant until the flux boils. You'll probably have to push the segments back together if they've separated from water evaporating from the flux; do this quickly to retain the heat.

10 Ball a chip of solder and pick it up with your solder pick, placing the solder on the joints one at a time. There are twelve joints where the segments meet: the six points around the edges and six more where the outer pieces meet the one in the middle. Be sure the solder is carefully placed exactly between each joint, or it may flow in the wrong direction. After all solder has been placed, heat the entire pendant until the solder flows neatly into the joints (C). Pickle and dry the piece.

11 For further decoration, add the six smallest tubes to the piece. To do this, flux in the grooves between the rounded segments, lay the piece on the soldering board, and place the smallest tubes into the grooves. Solder the tubes into place with medium solder (D), and then pickle and dry the pendant.

12 Sand both faces of the pendant flat on a sheet of 220-grit sandpaper; continue with 320-grit and 400-grit until the surfaces of both sides are smooth and even (E). The pendant should be about 3mm thick.

13 For the bail, use a piece of the 4mm tubing, and solder it to the top with easy solder (F).

14 After pickling and cleaning up any excess solder, this piece can be finished as desired. To reach the insides of the tubing, use a small steel brush or burr attachment on the flexible shaft to polish. Use a brass brush and a green scrub pad on the face to create a matte finish.

15 String on a chain or cord of your choice.

GALLERY

BASIC SOLDERING

1. MELISSA NECKLACE BY JAYE WOODSTOCK

sterling silver and beach stones

This necklace was created from sterling silver jump rings that were formed, joined, and soldered closed to create a continuous chain. *Photo by Robert Diamante*

2. PENDANT BY MELISSA FINELLI

sterling silver

This pendant was created from sterling silver tubing, sheet, and wire. Many techniques were used to make this piece, including dapping to flare the mouths of the tubing, forming, and soldering to connect the inner tubing to the pendant. *Photo by Peter Harris*

3. WAVE SET BY JENNIFER CHIN

sterling silver

I used sterling silver tubing and heavy-gauge round wire for all the pieces in this set. It was created similarly to the fizzy pendant project. The pieces of tubing and wire were all cut and soldered together in small segments and then soldered again to form a bracelet, pendant, and earrings. *Photo by Allen Bryan*

3

FORMING METAL:

OTHER FABRICATION TECHNIQUES

SCORING & BENDING

Creating form and dimension with raw materials such as sheet and wire can be as easy as bending it with your hands—but there are many other ways to bend, dome, and forge metals using hammers, dapping blocks, punches, and mandrels. A few of the many possibilities using these tools include creating spheres, boxes, and any other sort of form you wish.

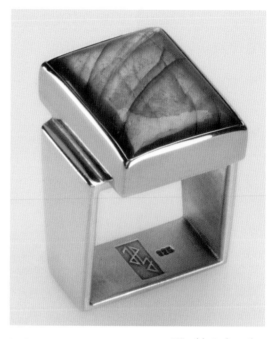

LABRADORITE RING BY JULIA GROOS, *18K gold, sterling silver, and labradorite*

Scoring and bending achieved solid 90° angles for a perfectly square ring band here. **PHOTO BY FREDRICK LEE**

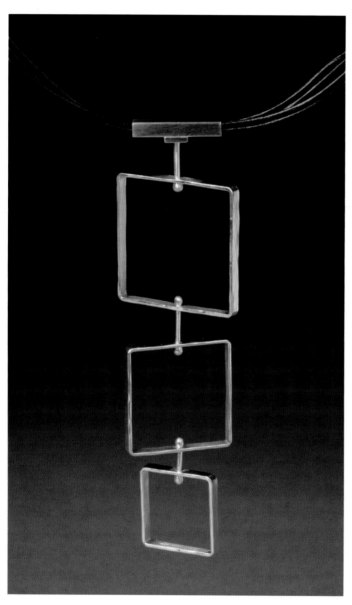

STERLING SILVER NECKLACE BY DONNA VEVERKA

Sterling silver wire has been bent and hammered into 90° angles to form squares in this pendant necklace. **PHOTO BY JAMES HULL**

LESSON 10

BENDING AN ANGLE

Scoring and bending are handy ways to create a clean angle with sheet metal. This technique is useful when making 90°-angled sides for boxes, cubes, and square ring bands.

WHAT YOU'LL NEED

Essential workbench tools (see page 22)
Basic soldering tool kit (see page 23)
Unannealed sheet metal, any metal
Scribe
Steel ruler
Square needle file

1 Begin by cutting your metal to the desired size, and determine where the angle will occur. Using a scribe and small metal ruler, score a straight line at that location. Be sure to make a deep line with the scribe, as it will provide the guide mark for filing in the next step.

2 Holding the metal firmly on your bench pin, use the angled edge of a square needle file to file a groove along the scribed line. Do this slowly and evenly, being careful not to file too much. You want the groove to *almost* reach the other side. Too much filing will cause a break when the metal is bent.

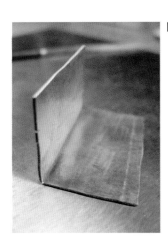

3 When you can start to see the filed lined from the back side, stop filing and gently bend the metal into the proper angle. Don't bend the metal back and forth, as this will cause weakening of the thin angle and breakage.

4 Flux and solder the inner angle with a small (2mm) chip of hard solder. A small chip placed in the angle will flow and fill the length of it, making the angle strong and unmovable.

FORGING

Forging is a technique used to change the shape and thickness of metal. Working metal against surfaces such as anvils and stakes with different hammers can create forms with volume and weight but also allow for delicate detail. The process of forging work-hardens the metal; this is why repeated blows with a hammer can create extremely strong yet intricate designs.

Anvils and forming blocks are stable surfaces that provide strong, smooth support when hammering or forging metal. Be sure to take care of these tools and keep their surfaces polished and smooth, as any imperfections will transfer to your metal when hammered.

Forging and planishing hammers are steel hammers used to shape metal. A planishing hammer has a smooth, polished surface that will move metal and also polish it at the same time. These hammers have one rounded side and a slightly curved side that cause the metal to spread and stretch with each blow.

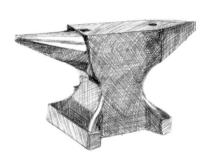

STERLING SILVER CUFF BRACELETS BY THERESA CARSON

After forging, texture was added with a flexible shaft attachment. **PHOTO BY RALPH GABRINER**

Shown from top to bottom: a stake, mini anvils, a larger anvil, and a planishing hammer.

USING A FORGING HAMMER

Essential workbench tools (see page 22)

Annealed sterling silver bar stock, round or square, 5–10mm thick

Anvil or steel block

Ear protection

Forging hammer

Planishing hammer

Using a forging hammer is an excellent way to change the shape of metal. Metal will become tough and work-hardened after being hammered, so re-annealing may be necessary to continue to shape the metal.

1. Position yourself comfortably so that you're sitting level with your anvil or hammering surface. You should not be bent over or reaching up to land hammer blows.

2. With ear protection on, hold your forging hammer loosely, and begin hammering where you want the metal to stretch. Don't grip the handle or use unnecessary force; let the hammer do the work for you. Be careful where your hammer lands, as the metal will move with every hit.

3. To taper the end of the rod, make sure the face of the hammer is perpendicular to the length of the rod, and then hammer and turn until the bar is rounded and thinner at the tip (A).

4. The metal will need to be annealed after a lot of hammering, as it will become work-hardened and unmovable (see annealing lesson on page 27). Listen for a pinging sound instead of a thud when hammering; this indicates the need to anneal.

5. Once you're satisfied with the tapered end, use the curved side of a planishing hammer to remove marks left from the forging hammer (B). Be careful not to overdo it, as the planishing hammer can further stretch the metal.

6. File and sand as desired.

DAPPING

Dapping is a technique used to create domed shapes and spheres in sheet metal. Dapping blocks and punches are used to form the domed depressions. Made of steel or wood, dapping blocks come in cube shapes or flat blocks and have various sizes of half-spheres depressed into them. The dapping punches are steel rods that fit into the dapping-block depressions and push and form the metal into the depressions.

A forming block is also used in conjunction with the dapping punches but utilizes the smooth handles of the punches laid on their sides to shape metal into the curved depressions of the block. Be sure to use a rawhide mallet against the handles so as not to damage the punches.

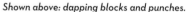

Shown above: dapping blocks and punches.

DENT RING BY MELISSA FINELLI, *sterling silver*

This ring was created using a dapping block and punch. Other techniques include ring-band forging and soldering. **PHOTO BY PETER HARRIS**

LESSON 12 — USING A DAPPING BLOCK

WHAT YOU'LL NEED

Essential workbench tools (see page 22)
Annealed sheet metal cut into any shape
Dapping block
Rawhide hammer

Dapping is a very useful way to add function and dimension to many jewelry pieces. This lesson covers the most basic dapping technique to create a domed shape in metal, using round shapes.

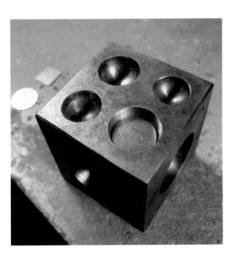

1 Select a depression in the dapping block that will create the desired dome, and place your metal into it.

2 Place a dapping punch that closely fits the size of the depression over the metal, and hammer it lightly with a rawhide mallet. The metal will be forced down. Be sure to aim your punch and blows at the edges of the metal first to ensure the metal is evenly domed. Move the dapping punch to the center, and continue hammering.

3 If necessary for your project, move the domed metal to a smaller depression to create a narrower shape, and repeat the process until you achieve your required shape.

DOMED PETAL EARRINGS

Precut disks from a jewelry supply retailer are handy for this project but not necessary. Cutting your own disks from sheet metal is great sawing practice and also gives you the opportunity to create shapes other than circles. Alternately, you can make these earrings with the domed sides facing up for a different look; simply turn the domed disks over when hooking them onto the jump rings.

A combination of dapping and piercing was used in creating the individual petal shapes for these sterling silver earrings. **PHOTO BY ALLEN BRYAN**

WHAT YOU'LL NEED

Essential workbench tools (see page 22)

Basic soldering tool kit (see page 23)

Sterling silver sheet, 24 gauge, or 40 precut 7mm silver disks

Flex shaft with drill attachment

Dapping block and punch

Rawhide mallet

Silver wire, 24 gauge

Silver wire, 22 gauge

Small mandrel

1 If you are making your own disks, cut forty (twenty for each earring) from the silver sheet, each 7mm in diameter (A). File the edges smooth and even. Anneal and dry the disks.

2 Drill one hole in each disk about 2mm in from the edge (B).

3 Place a disk into a depression in the dapping block. Place a dapping punch that closely fits the size of the depression over the metal disk, and hammer it lightly with a rawhide mallet. Repeat with the other disks.

4 Using the 24-gauge silver wire, make twenty small jump rings (refer to lesson 5 on page 43 if you need to). I used a mandrel the width of a needle-file handle to make the size I needed (C).

5 Put two disks onto a jump ring, concave sides facing outward and away from each other (D). Solder the jump ring closed with easy solder. Loop another jump ring between these first two disks, and add two more disks to that second jump ring (concave sides facing outward). You can continue to solder each link if desired, but it's not integral to the piece.

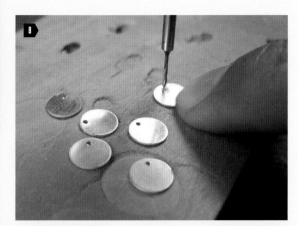

6 Continue until there are twenty disks total attached together on ten interlocking jump rings (two disks per ring). Repeat the process to create the other earring (E).

7 Using the 22-gauge silver wire, make two French earring wires (refer to lesson 6 on page 44), and attach each one to the first loop in each earring chain.

8 Finish by brushing all surfaces with a steel brush.

PROJECT

FORGED CHAIN NECKLACE

This project is a good introduction to chain making, which usually involves repeating steps over and over to create links. The chain is lovely on its own and can be embellished with a pendant if desired. Use one of the large center rings soldered to the top of a bezel to elegantly incorporate a focal point into the chain. This project uses 14-gauge wire, but you can select any gauge you like.

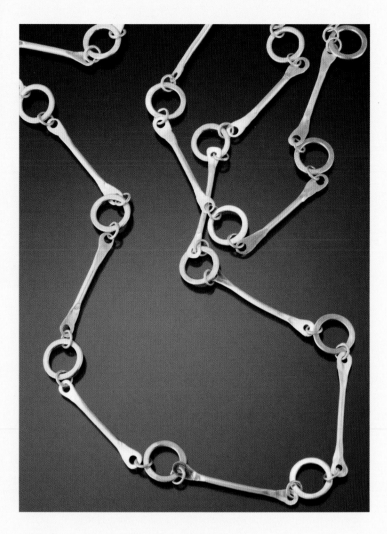

Forging and making jump rings are the main fabrication techniques used for this sterling silver chain. **PHOTO BY ALLEN BRYAN**

WHAT YOU'LL NEED

Essential workbench tools (see page 22)

Basic soldering tool kit (see page 23)

Annealed sterling silver wire, any gauge, approximately 20 inches in length

Chasing hammer

Flexible shaft with drill bit

Jeweler's saw

Hard and easy solder

1. Begin by forging the wire at one end using the back end of a chasing hammer (A). Be careful not to overstretch the metal; just create an even, flattened end.

2. Cut the wire 1 inch from the flattened end, and flatten the newly cut end to match what you did in step 1. Repeat steps 1 and 2 until you have a about twelve to sixteen of these pieces, or as many needed for the desired chain length. These will be the long links between the circular elements.

3. Round the ends of the links into uniform shape with a hand or needle file (B).

4. In each of the link ends, drill holes that are larger than your wire width to allow for movement in the chain (C).

5. With the same wire, create two sets of jump rings: large ones to go between each link and small ones to connect those large ones to the links. (Refer to lesson 5 on page 43 if you need to.) The length of your chain and number of links will determine the necessary amount of rings (D).

6. Solder closed the larger jump rings with hard solder, and pickle and clean up with fine, round needle files as needed.

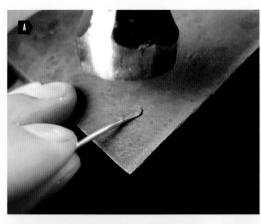

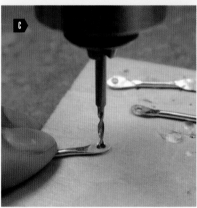

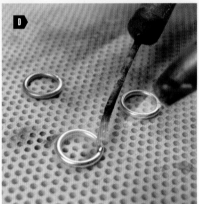

7 Use the round end of a chasing hammer to add a hammered texture to the large rings, and use the flat side to flatten them (E).

8 Use the smaller jump rings to connect the long wire links to the larger rings, attaching two links to each large ring (F). Continue until you have a long chain. Solder the smaller links closed with easy solder.

9 Create a simple S clasp to end the chain (see lesson 19 on page 134). Use one of the small jump rings to connect to the closed segment of the clasp, and solder it shut with easy solder.

   Alternately, you can make the chain long enough to slip over the head (at least 24 inches or longer).

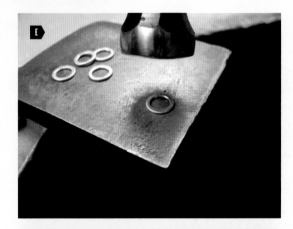

10 Clean up any excess solder and unintentional marks on your piece with needle files and sandpaper as desired.

11 Finish by brushing with a wet, soapy brass brush.

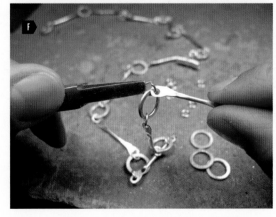

PROJECT
RETRO BRACELET

This simple bracelet has many steps and uses a simple, balled-wire linking element to join the rings. Its clasp is cut out of the ending ring to incorporate the closing mechanism into the design. The opening for the clasp is slightly smaller than the width of the clasp itself, making the closure secure. When making bracelets, always consider the clasp: Its design needs to enable easy opening and closing with one hand and be secure once it's clasped. The number and size of rings in this project create a 7-inch bracelet. To adjust the size, simply add or remove rings. The diameter of the rings can also be adjusted as desired.

The rings in this sterling silver retro bracelet were each formed around a round mandrel and hammered with the round end of a chasing hammer for added texture. **PHOTO BY ALLEN BRYAN**

WHAT YOU'LL NEED

Essential workbench tools (see page 22)

Basic soldering tool kit (see page 23)

Annealed sheet metal or 4mm-wide flat wire of your choice, 14–16 gauge

Rawhide mallet

Small mandrel

Hard and medium solder

Chasing hammer

Round wire of your choice, 18 gauge

1. Cut the sheet or flat wire into three segments, each 4mm wide by 2¼ inches long. These are the larger rings.

2. Cut four smaller secondary segments from the same sheet or flat wire, each 4mm wide by 1½ inches long. These are the smaller rings.

3. File the ends flat, and remove any saw marks from the sides.

4. Bend all of the segments, one at a time, over a ring mandrel (A), and use a rawhide mallet to shape the metal into a ring shape. Bend until the ends meet flush, with no space in between. Don't worry if the rings aren't perfectly round yet; they will be reshaped after the seams are soldered shut.

5. Working over a soldering board, solder the ends of each ring together with hard solder using the stick soldering method (B), and then pickle and dry these links.

6. Slide all the links, one at a time, on the ring mandrel, and hammer each lightly with the rawhide mallet all around until each is a perfectly round ring.

7. File any excess solder from the seam and sand all surfaces. Sand the edges clean and even by rubbing the rings facedown (edge down) on sandpaper in a figure-eight pattern.

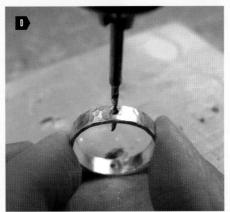

8 Create a hammered surface on each of the larger rings with the rounded side of a chasing hammer (C). (See page 92 for more on chasing.)

9 Drill two holes in the three large rings and in two of the smaller rings (D). The holes should be placed exactly opposite each other. Drill one hole only in the remaining two smaller rings; these rings will be used as the clasp and latch later on. Remember to use the center punch to create divots before drilling. Use the mandrel to hold each ring and as a support to punch against, because this will be easier than trying to hold each ring.

10 To create the clasp, a small segment must be removed from one of the small rings with the single hole. Use a measurement gauge or small ruler to determine the thickness of your metal. The section removed should be slightly smaller than the thickness of the ring and

approximately 2mm from the connecting wire (drilled hole) to create a secure clasp (E). After cutting, use a flat needle file to clean up the edges, removing any saw marks or burrs.

11 Cut six 1¼-inch pieces of the 18-gauge round wire.

12 Holding each of these cut pieces of wire in locking tweezers one at a time, light your torch, and heat one tip of each until a ball forms at the end (F). Be sure the ball is big enough that it won't slide through the drilled holes; melting approximately ¼ inch of the end of the wire should result in a 1–1.5mm round ball. Balling should happen very quickly. Set the wires aside to cool.

13 After the wires have cooled, take one of the larger rings and insert a balled wire from the inside. Thread the un-balled end through the outside of a smaller ring's hole. Pull the wire so that the ball is flush with the inside of the larger ring and the two rings are touching, with the wire pulled out past the opposite side of the smaller ring, and lay the two rings on the soldering board (G).

14 Light the torch, and heat the extending end until it balls down to meet the smaller ring's outside edge (H). Do not allow the ball to melt into the surface of the small ring; remove the flame as soon as the ball touches the ring. Repeat with the other two pieces, connecting the large ring to the small ring. The resulting balled wires will all be the same length, as the smaller ring is being used as a measurement tool: The wire can only be melted to the edge of the small ring, and all the small rings are the same size.

15 Connect all the segments together in the same manner, always inserting the 18-gauge balled wire into the inside hole of the large ring first and then into the outside hole of a small ring until you have a chain of alternating-size rings. Be sure the two smaller rings with the single holes are located on the ends. Pickle the bracelet.

16 Check the clasp mechanism, making sure the clasp ring slides into the latch ring with a small amount of resistance. If it is too small, file away metal until it is the correct size. If the opening is too large, squeeze the ring around a mandrel so that the ends are slightly closer together, being careful not to distort the shape. Finish by brushing the bracelet with a wet, soapy brass brush to polish the surface.

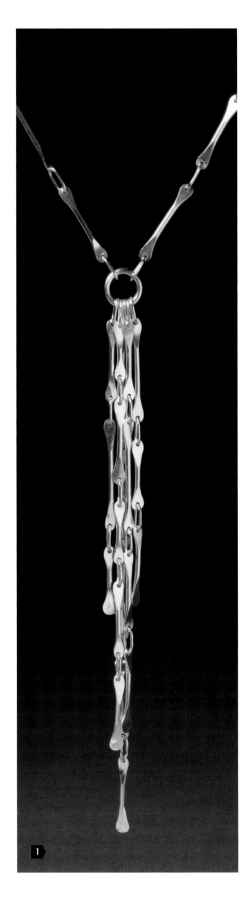

GALLERY

FORMING METAL

1. WATERFALL NECKLACE

BY DONNA VEVERKA

sterling silver

This necklace contains elements that have been forged. The ends of thick wires have been hammered and flared to create an interesting shape.

Photo by James Hull

2. FLORA NECKLACE

BY CHIHIRO MAKIO

sterling silver

Each segment of this sterling silver necklace is made up of twelve triangular sheets that have slits and slide together like paper. After the segments were soldered together, the edges were curled and hooked together using round pliers.

Photo by Ivo M. Vermeulen

3

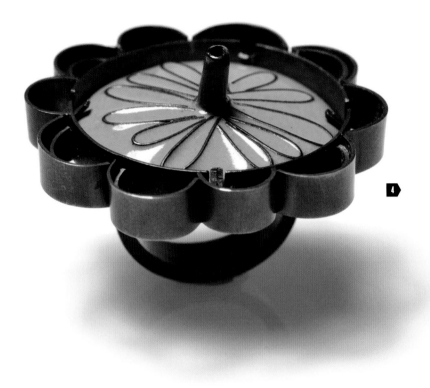

4

5

3. SWAN TEMPLE RING BY LISA CROWDER

sterling silver

Making use of dapping and forming, the top oval elements were domed slightly and soldered to the center wire. The ring band was formed with a mandrel and rawhide hammer and uses a rivet for closure. *Photo by Hap Sakwa*

4. RING BY LAUREN SCHLOSSBERG

sterling silver and enamel

Using pliers, segments of flat wire were bent and rounded and then soldered together into the shape of a flower. *Photo by Hap Sakwa*

5. FEELER RING BY MELISSA FINELLI

sterling silver

The bowl shape of this ring was formed with a dapping block and punch. The ring band was formed with a mandrel and hammered flat to emphasize its shape. *Photo by Peter Harris*

4

TEXTURES,
PATINAS
& FINISHING

CREATING TEXTURES WITH BASIC TOOLS

There are many ways to alter or embellish the surface of metals. Adding textures and patinas (which we'll get to later on in this chapter) can enhance interesting detail in your jewelry, giving it dimension and originality. Whether using hammers, a rolling mill, heat, or chemical oxidizers, consider the importance of this step in the jewelry-making process, and let your imagination guide you. To start, consider these two basic texturing techniques.

HAMMERED TEXTURES

Hammers are wonderful tools for creating a wide range of textures. The shape and variety of hammers make a difference, as does the surface on which a workpiece is hammered. On a steel base, metal expands outward when hammered. On a soft surface, such as a sandbag, metal has no resistance and will form a different shape. Hammering texture works best with annealed metal. Experiment with different hammers and surfaces to see what happens.

CUFF BRACELET BY LAURA PRESHONG, *sterling silver*

The texture of this bracelet was created using the ball end of a chasing hammer. The bracelet was then oxidized with liver of sulfur to emphasize the detail. **PHOTO BY THE ARTIST**

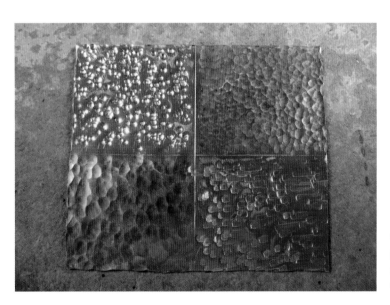

The textures on this copper sheet were created by hand with a variety of hammers. Pretextured sheet metal can be purchased through jewelry supply retailers (see Resources).

FLEXIBLE-SHAFT ATTACHMENTS

Using various attachments with the flexible shaft, you can create a tooled texture and pattern on your workpiece. A sanding disk is great for removing metal and excess solder, and used on its side, it can create interesting half-circle scratches. Brass- or steel-wire brushes can create a shiny surface. A hard rubber wheel will create small dimples resembling a hammered surface. Use diamond-tipped shaping burrs for a sparkling, sandblasted surface. Be sure to try out attachments on scrap metal before using them on a finished piece.

RING BY MELISSA FINELLI, *sterling silver and 18K gold*

Dapping, forging, and forming were all used in the process of creating this ring. The edges of the ring band and tips of the wire elements were hammered and oxidized. **PHOTO BY PETER HARRIS**

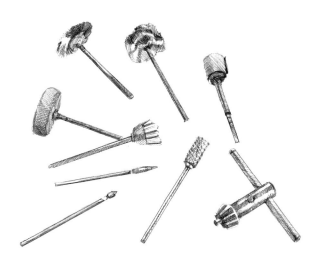

Various flex-shaft attachments.

Compare a few flex-shaft attachments and the resultant surface textures, from left to right: grinding cone, steel cylinder burr, polishing cone, round steel burr, and diamond-tipped burr.

SPLIT ELLIPSE RING BY THERESA CARSON, *sterling silver*

The decorative pattern on this piece was added using a steel burr on a flexible shaft. **PHOTO BY RALPH GABRINER**

CHASING

Chasing is an excellent way to embellish the surface of metal. For this technique, texture and design are essentially stamped into the surface of metal using steel hand tools. Many jewelers create their own chasing tools, punches, and stamps by carving shapes and textures into tool steel and tempering the metal, but a wide variety of premade chasing tools and stamps are available commercially.

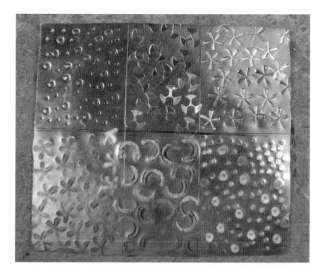

Copper sheet metal showing various stamped patterns created with chasing tools.

LESSON 13 ▸ CHASING A DESIGN

Be sure to experiment on nonprecious metal before using a stamp on your workpiece.

WHAT YOU'LL NEED

Sheet metal of your choice
Steel block
Chasing tools of your choice
Chasing hammer
Rawhide mallet

1 Place your sheet metal on the steel block. (You can use masking tape to keep the workpiece steady if desired.)

2 With one hand, position your chasing tool on the metal sheet, and with your other hand, tap the top of the tool with a chasing hammer once (A). For a deeper mark, a heavier hammer blow will do the job.

3 To flatten the sheet but not mar the surface, turn the metal over, and hammer it lightly with a rawhide mallet.

RETICULATION

Reticulation is a technique that uses heat to deliberately melt the surface of metal in a precise manner. The melted texture resembles a topographical map or wrinkled skin. Reticulation works best with sterling silver sheet that has a fine-silver exterior layer. Because of this silver-rich surface, the interior layer of the sterling silver contains more copper, which has a lower melting point than silver. When heated, the copper layer melts, deforming the surface and forming crests on it. After reticulation, metal is brittle, making it difficult to solder, and so a cold connection technique such as riveting is best when continuing a project.

Reticulated silver.

LESSON 14

RETICULATION

Practice is key with this technique. The results are unpredictable but can create very interesting, one-of-a-kind textures. Using a large sheet of metal—3 or 4 inches square—is a good idea, as results may vary throughout the workpiece.

WHAT YOU'LL NEED

Basic soldering tool kit (see page 23)
Sterling silver sheet metal, 18 gauge

1 Prepare the sterling silver metal by heating it to a dull red; then quench it in hot pickle, repeating at least four times until the surface is white. This process is called *depletion gilding,* which is also used to cover firescale. Heating and quenching bring fine silver up to the surface, while the interior layer now contains more copper. Clean the metal with a soapy, wet brass brush or green scrub pad.

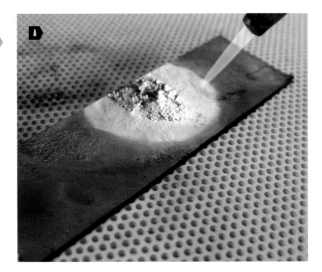

2 Before placing your metal on the work surface, preheat the area to ensure even heating, and then place the metal on the heated surface.

3 Use a medium-soft flame to heat the metal; increase the flame as the metal begins to collapse.

4 As the metal begins to pucker, move the flame across the sheet (A). Holding the flame too long in one place will create a hole in the sheet. Watch the surface very closely. You can control the puckering by moving your flame.

5 Pickle, rinse, and dry your reticulated metal.

EMBOSSING WITH A ROLLING MILL

Rolling mills are excellent tools that can be used for many purposes, among them to imprint and press metal. They have two round rollers with a space in between that can be adjusted to any desired position. Turning the long handle on the side pushes the metal through the rollers and, consequently, makes the metal thinner or imprints it with a texture. (Rolling mills can also come with specialty rollers for wire and patterned textures.)

Rolling mills aren't an essential tool and can be a bit of an investment, but they're invaluable for creating texture or rolling out your own sheet metal or wire. If you don't have a rolling mill, you can imprint texture using a hammer: Simply lay your texturizing material over annealed sheet and hammer gently against a steel block. The resulting pattern will be less even than the pattern from a rolling mill—but all the more interesting! Experiment with materials, and see what happens.

BETH ANN EARRINGS BY JAYE WOODSTOCK, *sterling silver and beach stones*

The interesting texture on these earrings was created using metal screen and a rolling mill. The metal was rolled through the mill several times for an overlapping pattern. **PHOTO BY ROBERT DIAMANTE**

Used for creating texturing and milling wire and sheet, a rolling mill is a useful tool. If rolling ferrous metal through the mill, always use a brass or copper sheet between the ferrous metal and the rollers to protect them from damage.

A rolling mill in use.

EMBOSSING TEXTURE IDEAS

Window screen	Coarse fabric
Dried flowers and leaves	Heavy-grit sandpaper
Wire	Paper with cut out design
Pattern pierced and sawed out of sheet	Broken saw blades

ROLLING TEXTURE

Be sure your metal is annealed and soft to allow the texture to be easily imprinted. Before beginning, cut your sheet to accommodate your design and fit through the mill's rollers. If your texture source is made from a ferrous metal (one containing iron), put a nonferrous sheet (brass or copper) on top of it as it goes through the mill to protect the rollers from damage. Ferrous metals can be harder than the mill's rollers and will imprint texture onto the rollers if used without a protective layer.

WHAT YOU'LL NEED

Basic soldering tool kit (see page 23)

Nonferrous sheet metal of your choice

Texture source (see box for ideas)

Nonferrous metal sheet (brass or copper) to protect rollers if using a ferrous metal texture source

Rolling mill

1. Anneal the metal to be imprinted. Place the texture source on top of the metal, and cover with nonferrous metal sheet if the texture source is a ferrous material.

2. Open the rollers, and place the sheets between them. Adjust the size of the opening (turning the handle so that the opening is wider or smaller) so that the metal fits snugly (A). Remove the metal, and turn the mill's handle one half-rotation to bring the rollers closer together.

3. Place the sheets in the roller once more, and roll the metal through the rollers (B). The handle should be slightly difficult to turn but not immovable.

4. Rolled metal will be work-hardened after going through the mill, so reanneal your sheet before rolling again or hammering flat.

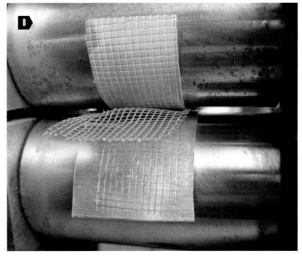

PATINAS

A patina is a fine coating of oxide on the surface of metal. There are many patina recipes and techniques used to add color to and blacken metal, many of which are very toxic. Be sure to work in a well-ventilated area, and do your research before beginning any patina experiment.

The most common chemical used to blacken silver and copper is *liver of sulfur*; patina results range from gold to red, blue to purple, and finally black, depending on the length of time metal is exposed to it. Applying any chemical patina should be done after all hot processes are completed.

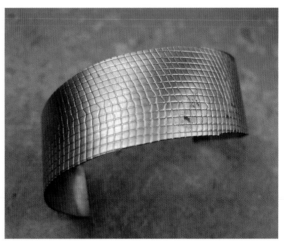

A simple way to oxidize metal is by heating it with a torch. As seen on this example, a beautiful range of colors can be achieved on copper with this intentional heat oxidation. To seal the oxidation, apply a clear lacquer or wax over the surface oxidation.

The top image shows oxidized silver dipped in liver of sulfur solution, and below that is the finished result after being brushed with a brass brush.

TEETH PENDANT BY MELISSA FINELLI, *sterling silver and 18K gold*

This necklace was oxidized with liver of sulfur; the piece contains both silver and gold, but just the silver has been oxidized, as gold is not affected by liver of sulfur. **PHOTO BY PETER HARRIS**

TOP: **NECKLACE BY THERESA CARSON,** *sterling silver*

This necklace was oxidized before texture and pattern were added. A steel burr was used to create the pattern at the top, and steel wool was used for the brushed surface on the bottom. **PHOTO BY RALPH GABRINER**

BOTTOM: **MULTI-BALL NECKLACE BY LAUREN SCHLOSSBERG,** *sterling silver and glass beads*

The sterling silver elements in this piece were oxidized using liver of sulfur. To bring out the shine, the beads were brushed with a brass brush after oxidation. **PHOTO BY HAP SAKWA**

POLISHING

Finishing takes patience. It is an important step. Be sure not to skip it, as this final process is integral to the overall quality of your workpiece. After filing and sanding off all unintentional marks, excess solder, and rough edges, a final finishing—or polishing—step will bring out the beauty of the metal.

Use steel or brass brushes to achieve a shiny finish. Metal brush attachments on the flexible shaft are great for getting into tight spaces. For matte finishes, green scrub pads and steel wool create lovely brushed surfaces.

Tumblers loaded with polishing mediums will create uniform shiny surfaces; use stainless steel shot for maximum polish. Delicate chains or pieces with fragile wire components should not be polished in a tumbler, as they may become damaged or tangled.

Polishing machines are useful for creating even, professional finishes on metal. Essentially just a motor with two rotating spindles at its sides, a polishing machine uses buffing wheels made from many different materials (for example, steel and brass brushes, rubber, or natural bristles) to create various finishes on metal. Muslin, chamois leather, and felt buffs are used with polishing compounds to create a very shiny finish on metal.

For a beginning jeweler, a polishing machine isn't an essential tool, as it is expensive and many of the same finishes can be achieved with a flexible shaft using the same polishing compounds and small buffing wheels.

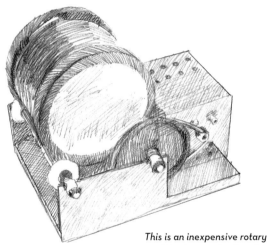

This is an inexpensive rotary tumbler that can be found at any jeweler's supply retailer or hobby shop.

AVOCADO NECKLACE BY HILARY HACHEY, *sterling silver*

This necklace was created with tubing and flat wire bent into various shapes. Components were then soldered together using the wire soldering method. The piece has an oxidized top surface that was polished to a smooth, shiny finish using a polishing buff on a polishing machine. **PHOTO BY HAP SAKWA**

LESSON 15 〉 CREATING A MIRROR FINISH

To achieve a mirror finish—the shiniest finish of them all—polishing buffs and compounds are needed. Like sandpaper, polishing compounds remove metal to polish surfaces and should be used in order of abrasiveness. For a mirror finish, a prepolishing compound called *tripoli* is applied to a buffing wheel and used first to prepare the surface of the metal. Brown tripoli is moderately abrasive and can be used for any metals. White diamond is another form of tripoli that is used with silver and gold; it has a finer abrasive polish. After tripoli has been applied, *rouge* should be used for a final polish. There are many varieties of rouge: Red rouge can be used for silver, gold, copper, and brass. Green rouge is used for white gold, platinum, and nickel. Black rouge is used for silver. Yellow rouge is used for platinum. Always use a dedicated polishing wheel for each compound.

If you're considering polishing any of the projects in this book, a combination of white diamond and red rouge is best. When using a polishing machine, be sure to wear proper eye protection and to tie back any loose hair or clothing.

ROSE QUARTZ RING BY JULIA GROOS, *sterling silver and rose quartz*

To create a mirror finish on this ring, a polishing machine was used for the ring's final finishing step. White diamond compound was used to prepolish the surface, followed by red rouge for the last polish. **PHOTO BY FREDRICK LEE**

WHAT YOU'LL NEED

Metal to be polished (sterling silver or base metal)

Polishing compounds: tripoli (white diamond) and red rouge

Polishing machine

3 cotton buffing wheels

1 Turn on the polishing machine, and place a buffing wheel on the moving spindle. The force of the rotation will pull the buffing wheel into place.

2 Hold the block of tripoli compound against the wheel to coat the cotton until it is significantly covered.

3 Holding the metal to be polished firmly in both hands, rub the metal onto the wheel about halfway down from the center (A). At this level, the metal is less likely to fly out of your hands and is easier to hold on to.

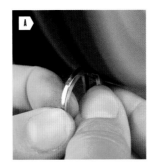

4 Firmly rub all desired surfaces, making sure to not pause for too long on one spot; the polishing compound removes metal to polish it, and the surface can be easily damaged.

5 Repeat steps 1 through 4 with the rouge compounds, using a new cotton buffing wheel for the rouge.

6 To clean the metal after polishing, use a soft-bristled toothbrush with dish soap and hot water. Don't use anything abrasive to clean the metal, as it may scratch the mirror surface.

PROJECT
CHASED BANGLE

This bracelet can be made with any size square or rectangular wire, which is often referred to as sizing stock, because it is used to make specific sizes of rings, bracelets, and so on. Thicker-gauge wire will make a heavier bangle. Round and half-round wires are also great for bangles, but this project uses square wire for ease of chasing a pattern on the flat surfaces. Oxidizing the metal will bring out your design; you can blacken the piece with liver of sulfur and finish the surface as desired.

I created the pattern on this bracelet using chasing tools and stamps. After I added the texture, I oxidized the metal with liver of sulfur and sanded it with 400-grit sandpaper to bring out the design detail. **PHOTO BY ALLEN BRYAN**

WHAT YOU'LL NEED

Essential workbench tools (see page 22)

Basic soldering tool kit (see page 23)

Square or rectangular sizing stock, 4 x 1.5mm

Bracelet mandrel

Hard solder

Rawhide hammer

Chasing tools

Liver of sulfur (optional)

1 Begin by sawing a length of the square wire. This project uses a segment measuring 8 inches long by 4mm wide by 1.5mm thick to fit over an average-size hand. The length will vary depending on the size of bangle you require; adding an inch to your regular bracelet size will give you your bangle size, but you may have to increase the length if your hand is large.

2 File the ends flush. With a bracelet mandrel and pliers, bend the wire into a round shape. Don't worry if it's not perfectly round yet; it will be reshaped later. (Also see step 7.)

3 After checking that the ends meet perfectly (A), create tension between the ends by pushing them together until they overlap inward. Once this tension has been created, the ends will stay together nicely. Open the joint, and line up the ends.

4 Solder the joint with hard solder, and then pickle and dry.

5 Reshape the bracelet into a circle on a round bracelet mandrel by hammering on all sides with a rawhide hammer (B).

6 Use files and sandpaper to remove any excess solder outside the seam. File and round the edges as desired. Sand all surfaces with 400-grit sandpaper, getting rid of any unwanted marks or scratches.

7 Place the bangle back onto the bracelet mandrel, line up the chasing tool, and strike with the chasing hammer. Repeat until you have the desired pattern. Remove the bangle from the mandrel, and chase the sides, as well, if you like (C).

   Alternately, this step may be done after step 2, while the metal is still in a flat shape, though the chasing pattern may be distorted after you then hammer the metal into its round bangle configuration.

8 Finish with a steel brush or green scrub pad.

EMBOSSED CUFF LINKS

This project uses the rolling mill to create an embossed design on the metal. Experiment with different texturizing elements to see what kinds of patterns you can make. These cuff links use commercially made link back findings; other styles of cuff link backs swivel on rivets and also work well with the design. Cuff link backs can be purchased through jewelry supply retailers.

Embossing gives these sterling silver cuff links their surface texture, while dapping creates the domed shape. **PHOTO BY ALLEN BRYAN**

WHAT YOU'LL NEED

Essential workbench tools (see page 22)

Basic soldering tool kit (see page 23)

Annealed sterling silver sheet metal, 22-24 gauge

Material to create emboss texture

Rawhide hammer

Commercially made cuff link backs

Liver of sulfur (optional)

Rolling mill

1 Texture the metal with your chosen material in the rolling mill. I used some steel window screen to create texture (A). Reanneal and hammer the metal flat with a rawhide hammer if needed. Remember to place a brass sheet over any ferrous texture source to protect the mill's rollers.

2 Cut out two 11mm-square pieces from the now-textured sheet.

3 With the rawhide hammer, gently bend each square around a mandrel to create a slight curve.

Alternately, you can also shape the squares with a dapping block and punch, though loss of embossed texture may occur. To do this, insert a square into a depression in the dapping block, and gently tap the punch until the square is domed into a pillow shape. Repeat with the other square, making them as similar as possible.

4 Lightly sand the corners of each curved square to create a flat surface onto which the bottom sheet will be soldered (B).

5 Cut out two more squares from the sheet, measuring slightly longer than the first two. File any burrs, and working on a soldering board, place each domed square on top of a flat square. The flat pieces should extend slightly past the corners of the curved pieces. Flux and solder the two pieces together (C); then pickle and dry them.

6 Remove the ends of the flat section with your jeweler's saw, and then file the ends until the joint is flush and the seam is clean (D).

7 Connect the cuff link backs; I used commercially made cuff link backs. Preflow easy solder onto each back, and use locking tweezers to hold the back while heating (E). Pickle and rinse the cuff links.

8 Clean and polish the links with a soapy wet brass brush.

PROJECT
RETICULATED EARRINGS

Reticulation (see page 93) is a challenging technique but, when done successfully, will create beautiful, one-of-a-kind texture. Reticulated metal is brittle after heating, so rivets and cold connections form the additional decoration here. A shape template for this project can be found on page 154, but you can create any shape you like. The earrings created in the project are 2 inches long and ½ inch wide, and use 14K gold tubing.

Finished sterling silver and 14K gold reticulated earrings. **PHOTO BY ALLEN BRYAN**

WHAT YOU'LL NEED

Essential workbench tools (see page 22)

Basic soldering tool kit (see page 23)

Reticulated silver sheet metal

3mm tubing of your choice

Flaring tool

Chasing hammer

Silver round wire, 19 gauge

1 Reticulate your silver sheet metal (see lesson 14 on page 93 if needed). Be sure you have enough usable surface to create a pair of earrings.

2 After pickling and cleaning the reticulated sheet, cut two desired earring shapes out of it with a jeweler's saw (A).

3 With a drill attachment in your flex shaft, drill a hole in each shape at the point where you want to attach an earring wire. Drill three more holes in each earring, placing them as desired. Be sure to use a drill bit that is the same size as the tubing.

4 To create split rivets with tubing, hold the tubing firmly (use pliers or a ring clamp to avoid cutting into your fingers with the saw), and saw slots (like cross-hairs) in one end (B). Cut the tube into a length that accommodates the thickness of your reticulated sheet, turn the cut piece over, and saw slots in the other end. Repeat to make as many rivets as needed for your design. This piece uses eight rivets total: two tube rivets for attaching the earring wires and six decorative split rivets.

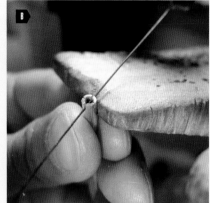

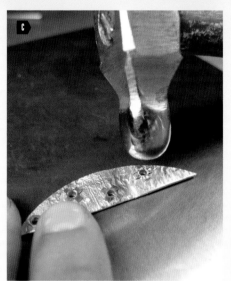

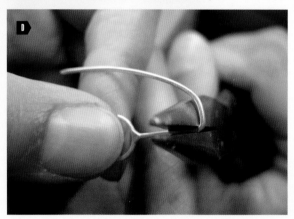

Longer sawed slots will create a more decorative split rivet. Experiment with length and number of sawed slots to discover other results. Also, consider if the design will be viewed from only one side; the rivet will only need one decorative embellishment if that's the case.

5 Begin flaring one end of each rivet with chain-nose pliers or a flaring tool. One at a time, insert each rivet into a drilled hole, flare the slots (or plain tube if you're not making split rivets) on the other side, and flip over. Repeat until all rivets are in place.

6 Flip the earrings over, hammer the flared rivets carefully with the chasing hammer (C), and sand as needed with 400-grit sandpaper. Be careful not to mar or flatten the reticulated silver surface.

7 To make the French earring wires, create two large jump rings with the 19-gauge wire. Add one to each earring through its top riveted hole. Clamp the jump ring in some locking tweezers using a third-hand soldering aid. With the jump ring opening positioned upward, solder a 2-inch length of 19-gauge wire to this point on each jump ring.

8 Grasp the wire ½ inch up from where it meets the jump ring. With half-round pliers, bend the wire back toward the back side of the earring to form a gentle curve (D). Lightly hammer the wire to work-harden it. Sand the end of the wire into a smooth rounded shape. Repeat with the other earring.

9 Give the earrings a finish of your choice. I used a steel brush for a shiny surface.

1

2

3

GALLERY
TEXTURES & PATINAS

1. MOON CUFF BRACELET
BY PETRA SEIBERTOVA

copper

This hollow-form bracelet's texture was created by chasing, forming, hammering, and carving. The textured pieces were formed into curved shapes and soldered to the inner ring. The bracelet was then oxidized to bring out the intricate detail.
Photo by Adam Krauth

2. DOT PIN BY LISA CROWDER

sterling silver and 18K bi-metal

This pin was created using dapping and riveting. The surface was oxidized and then brushed with a brass brush for added shine. *Photo by Hap Sakwa*

3. NECKLACE BY THERESA CARSON

sterling silver

This pendant has been oxidized and polished to bring out the detail on the inside of the "clam shell" element. Detail was added using a sharp steel hand tool to scratch lines into the oxidation.
Photo by Ralph Gabriner

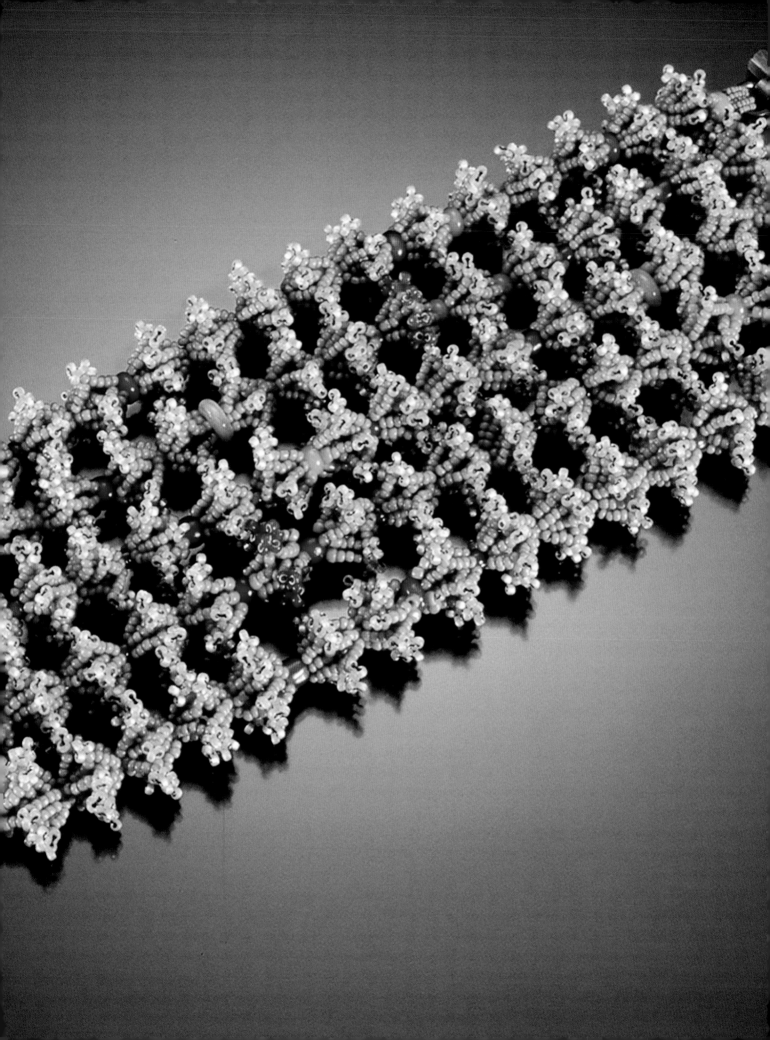

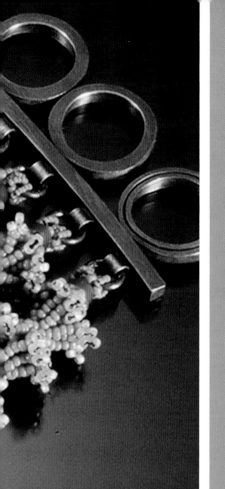

5

ADDING
STONES
& BEADS

GEMSTONES VS. OTHER MATERIALS

Incorporating gemstones and beads can add color, dimension, and focus to jewelry. Gemstones are available in a wide range of colors, cuts, and sizes, and prices range from the very cheap to the wildly expensive, depending on factors such as rarity, durability, and popularity. For example, the *precious* gemstones (diamonds, sapphires, rubies, and emeralds) are usually very expensive, while *semiprecious* stones (such as amethysts, tourmaline, topaz, and peridot, just to name a few) are often much more accessible in price.

It's important to consider all these qualities when buying stones as well as how stones will be set. Fragile, porous stones, such as opals and pearls, need to be protected in a setting and work best in jewelry that won't receive much impact, such as earrings and pendants.

Harder gemstones, such as diamonds, sapphires, and rubies, are very durable and work well in rings and bracelets. Semi- and nonprecious stones also range in durability and color choices, and they are excellent alternatives to pricier stones. Be sure to do your research before purchasing.

As well as durability in a setting, it is important to consider the fragility of gemstones worn on the body that are exposed to destructive elements such as detergents, perfumes, and lotions. Stones such as turquoise, pearls, jade, and opals are delicate and can be discolored and damaged easily by exposure to household chemicals. When deciding what kind of stones to use in a design, keep this in mind to create pieces that will be both beautiful and long-lasting.

Various semiprecious cabochons, faceted stones, and beads.

PENDANT BY LAURA PRESHONG, *sterling silver and blown glass*

This pendant uses blown glass set in sterling silver. The glass is held in the setting by prongs, allowing the sides and tops of each piece to be seen. **PHOTO BY ALLEN BRYAN**

RINGS BY JULIA GROOS, *18K gold, Indian star rubies, diamonds*

The main stones in these rings are bezel-set star rubies. The diamond accents on the right-hand ring are set in bezels created from tubing. **PHOTO BY FREDRICK LEE**

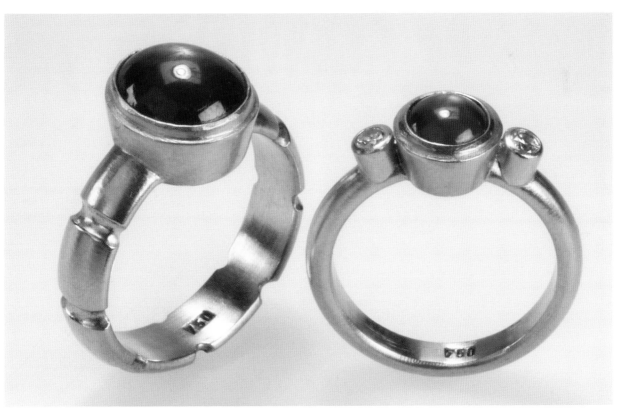

The terms *cabochon* and *faceted* refer to the cut of a stone. Cabochons are gemstones cut with a flat base and a smooth, rounded top. They're most often found in circular or oval shapes. Setting a cabochon stone in a jewelry piece usually involves a bezel (a small collar of metal that surrounds the stone). It is pushed against the rounded sides of the cabochon to keep the stone secure. A cabochon's wider, flat bottom sits inside the bezel collar, locking it inside.

Faceted gemstones have flat and angled sides that reflect light and sparkle. They're available in many shapes: round, princess, emerald, oval, marquise, and pear to name a few. Precious gemstones, such as diamonds, emeralds, and sapphires, are most often faceted to enhance their beauty. Faceted stones are often set in prong settings to allow light to shine through all sides and increase a stone's sparkle and brilliance. They also can be set in bezel-style settings, though light refraction will be more limited.

Materials such as glass, plastic, bone, stone, and wood are often set into jewelry. An object's "preciousness" is not necessarily related to what it is made of. Nonprecious items are often much more beautiful than faceted stones and can be much more versatile. You can drill through stone, bone, and wood, and plastic can be heated and reshaped. Glass and resin can be sanded and polished.

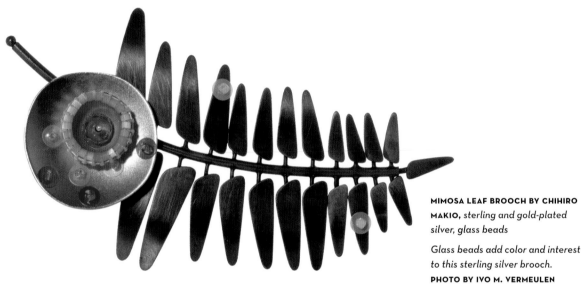

MIMOSA LEAF BROOCH BY CHIHIRO MAKIO, *sterling and gold-plated silver, glass beads*

Glass beads add color and interest to this sterling silver brooch. **PHOTO BY IVO M. VERMEULEN**

PIN BY TAMI RODRIG, *sterling silver, paint, beads, paper, and resin*

This pin makes use of many nonprecious materials—glass beads, paper, elastic cord, paint—set in resin. **PHOTO BY ROBERT DIAMANTE**

NECKLACE BY LAURA PRESHONG, *sterling silver and glass*

The bezels fully encircle the pieces of glass here to hold each one in place. Compare this to the setting of the pendant on page 111, by the same artist. **PHOTO BY ALLEN BRYAN**

RING BY LAURA PRESHONG, *sterling silver and blown glass*

A bezel setting is used here to hold the blown glass securely in place. **PHOTO BY ALLEN BRYAN**

SETTING STONES

To incorporate stones, beads, or other materials into your jewelry pieces, you'll need a few specific setting tools to set stones and objects in their metal holders, or settings. Two common settings are bezels and prongs, and there are other various constructions. Following the general tool descriptions here, the next two lessons will explore how to use setting tools in more detail to set stones in bezel and flush settings.

Bezel pushers gently push metal around a stone, pinching it in place. Bezel rollers roll the remaining bezel so that all surrounding material is flush with the stone. After a stone is secured in a bezel, you can use a burnishing tool to rub and smooth the metal around the lip of the stone. This polishing tool will work to harden bezels and smooth any rough edges. A ring clamp will keep a tight grip on a band while the bezel is being pushed around a stone.

ESSENTIAL STONE-SETTING TOOLS

- ☐ Ring clamp
- ☐ Bezel pusher
- ☐ Bezel roller
- ☐ Burnisher

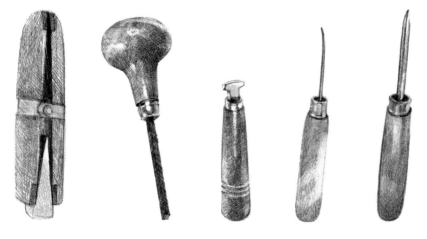

Shown from left to right: ring clamp, bezel pusher, bezel roller, and two burnishers.

TOO HIGH **TOO LOW** **IDEAL**

Proper bezel height is key to a successfully set stone. If your bezel is too tall, the metal will buckle and pinch when pushed around the stone, because there is excess metal. A bezel that is too short won't hold a stone securely, and the stone will fall out of the setting. An ideal bezel is approximately half to two-thirds of the height of the stone.

ADDING STONES & BEADS

A bezel being smoothed around a stone using a burnisher. Using this tool after a stone is set will smooth, polish, and even out the edge of a bezel.

JESSIE BRACELETS BY JAYE WOODSTOCK, *sterling silver and beach stones*

These bracelets contain beach stones bezel-set in sterling silver. The texture was achieved by embossing a metal screen pattern into the silver with a rolling mill. **PHOTO BY ROBERT DIAMANTE**

MAKING A BEZEL

One of the most commonly used settings, a bezel is a strip of metal that surrounds and holds a stone. The metal is pushed against the sides of the stone, creating pressure that holds the stone in place. No matter the shape, bezels work with cabochons, faceted stones, or any object for which you wish to make a setting. We'll use a cabochon here. Bezels can be made with or without a full back underneath the stone, depending on the design and shape of the object to be set.

WHAT YOU'LL NEED

Essential workbench tools (see page 22)

Basic soldering tool kit (see page 23)

Fine-silver bezel wire, 24–26 gauge

Sheet metal (silver or base metal), any gauge

Cabochon, any shape

Bezel pusher or bezel rocker

Burnisher

BEZEL SETTING TIPS

☐ Always push the bezel around the stone from alternating sides for even setting. (Don't begin by just going in a consecutive circular motion around the bezel.)

☐ Make sure the workpiece construction is secure before setting the stone.

☐ Use beeswax to remove a crooked stone by first warming the wax in your hand to soften it slightly and then pressing the wax onto the stone and gently pulling it out of the setting. Another stone-removal method when you are just checking the stone's fit in its bezel is to place a long piece of dental floss across the bezel, place the stone in the bezel (so that the floss is under the stone with ends sticking out), and then pull both ends of the floss to pop out the stone.

☐ Burnish the bezel to polish and toughen the metal after the stone is in place.

1 Lay the stone flat on your work surface, and wrap the bezel wire around it to determine the approximate length of wire needed. The bezel should be tall enough to wrap under the bottom edge of your stone but not so tall that it will buckle or pucker when pushed around the stone.

2 Cut or saw the bezel wire using flush cutters or a saw. Refit the bezel, and trim as needed to make sure the bezel fits around the stone without any space or overlap at the ends. Place the ends of the bezel together so that they meet perfectly, as pictured, and squeeze with some flat-nose pliers to ensure a tight fit.

3 Flux the seam and solder using one small chip of hard solder, as pictured. Pickle and rinse the bezel, and clean up any extra solder from the joint using needle files. Finish with fine-grit sandpaper.

4 Place your bezel on a small mandrel, and hammer gently with a rawhide mallet until it is round. Sand the bottom of your bezel so that it lies flat. Check the fit against the stone, which should fit in the bezel without being forced and shouldn't be able to move once inside.

   Then remove the stone, and place the bezel onto the sheet metal. Using a scribe or a thin marker, trace a circle around the bezel that is at least 2mm larger in diameter than the bezel itself and cut the metal out with a saw. This is your back sheet; cutting it a little larger than the bezel will make soldering easier, giving you a surface to lay a chip of solder onto around the bezel. Flux the sheet and place the bezel onto it. Lay a segment of medium solder on the inside side perimeter of the bezel. Be sure it is touching both the bezel wall and the bottom sheet. Heat and solder the bezel to the sheet, concentrating heat on the bottom sheet, inside and outside of the bezel. Pickle and rinse the metal.

5 Trim any excess sheet metal from the bottom of your bezel using a saw or shears if the metal is thin. Using files and sandpaper, clean up the surface to a fine finish.

   At this point, complete any other soldering processes, such as soldering the bezel to a ring band or adding a jump ring; any hot technique or use of abrasives and chemicals must be completed before setting the stone.

6 To set the stone, place it in the bezel, and use a bezel pusher or roller to gently push the bezel against the stone. Start at the top at the 12 o'clock position, then move to the 6 o'clock position, then to 3 o'clock, and finally to 9 o'clock. Doing this ensures that the stone is held evenly within the bezel and prevents creases in the bezel itself.

   Push the rest of the bezel (in between the spots you just pushed) over the stone with the pusher or roller. Using a burnisher, rub the bezel to make sure the stone is snug and doesn't move. Be careful not to touch the stone, as a metal burnisher can easily scratch soft stones.

FLUSH STONE SETTING

Flush setting is an excellent way to add brilliant-cut stones to a workpiece. *Flush* indicates here that the table of the stone (see diagram below) is even with the surface of the metal in a modified bezel, while the girdle of the stone sits beneath the surface. This is achieved by creating a "seat" (a small concave depression) for the stone in the surface of the metal using a burr. Burrs are sharp, steel tools used with the flexible shaft for many operations, some of which include grinding, precision carving, and cutting seats in metal for stones.

Burrs are available in many shapes and types. This project uses a 90° hart burr to cut a seat for a small faceted stone. When using a 90° hart burr to cut a seat in metal, use a lightly smaller-sized burr than the stone to be set. So, for example, if the stone is 3mm, use a 2.8mm burr. You can always grind out a larger seat if you find that the seat is too small for the stone. The stone is then placed into the seat, and a tiny amount of metal is pushed around its edges to secure it. This technique works well when using very small faceted stones. The setting is clean and modern and is a great way to incorporate stones into the surface of a workpiece.

WHAT YOU'LL NEED

Essential workbench tools (see page 22)

Faceted round stone, .05–3.5mm in diameter

Sheet metal of your choice, at least .75mm thicker than width of stone from table to girdle

90° hart burr, approximately .1 mm smaller than stone

MILKY WAY RING BY JULIA GROOS, *18K gold and diamonds*
The diamonds in this ring have been set using the flush-setting technique. **PHOTO BY FREDRICK LEE**

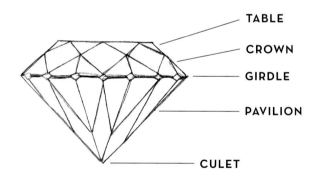

TABLE

CROWN

GIRDLE

PAVILION

CULET

This diagram shows the parts of a round faceted gemstone. The purpose of a faceted cut is to display a gem's brilliance to the fullest extent. Light entering the gemstone highlights the angled cuts, giving the stone sparkle and luster.

1. Position the stone on your sheet metal in the desired spot, and mark the metal where the center of the stone will fall.

2. Using a small drill bit (less than half the diameter of the stone), drill a hole through the metal on that center mark (A).

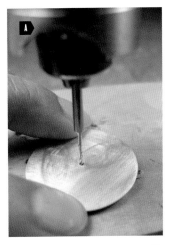

3. Using a 90° hart burr in a flex shaft that's slightly smaller than the stone, slowly cut the seat into the metal until the girdle of the burr is flush with the metal's surface (B). Use Bur-Life or beeswax on the burr to lubricate and cool the cutting area. Be careful not to cut the seat too large.

4. Lay the stone into its seat, and press it into place with a brass pusher. The stone should snap in and fit snugly in its seat.

5. Using a setting tool, push the metal around the sides of the stone (C). It can be helpful to create a small, rounded groove around the stone as an access point for the tool when pushing metal onto the stone. Repeat around the edges until the stone is secure. Using a burnisher, rub the metal down and over the edge of the stone.

6. To test the security of the setting, put any attachment on your flexible shaft, turn it on, and hold the attachment against the workpiece. As it rotates and vibrates the piece, watch carefully to see if the stone rattles or moves (D).

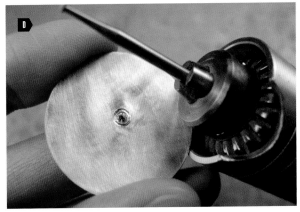

PROJECT
CABOCHON BROOCH

This project embellishes a simple bezel-set stone with decorative chasing detail and silver balls made from wire. An opaque stone works better in this setting than a clear a one, because the metal backing sheet behind the stone can distort a clear stone's color. Be sure to play with the shape of the backing sheet. I've created a star shape reminiscent of a sheriff's badge, but you can cut scalloped edges, flower petals, or anything else that inspires you.

The stone in this sterling silver brooch is an oval cabochon turquoise measuring 25mm x 18mm. **PHOTO BY ALLEN BRYAN**

WHAT YOU'LL NEED

Essential workbench tools (see page 22)

Basic soldering tool kit (see page 23)

Cabochon or any flat-bottomed stone, any size or shape

Silver bezel wire, 24–26 gauge

Sterling silver sheet metal, 22–24 gauge

Silver wire, 18 and 22 gauge

Chasing tools

Chasing hammer

Bezel pusher

Bezel roller

Burnisher

1 Create the bezel for your cabochon (see lesson 17 on page 116 if needed). For the embellished backing, lay the cabochon on the sheet metal and trace around it. Then draw the star shape around this cabochon shape, which should be centered in the middle of the star shape. Put the cabochon aside, and cut out the star shape with a jeweler's saw. Don't solder the bezel collar to the sheet yet.

2 Create silver balls with segments of the 22-gauge wire. Since I have eight points on my star, I cut eight 1-inch pieces of 22-gauge wire. Heat the pieces of wire until they melt neatly into balls (A); then allow them to cool and pickle them.

3 Flux the tips of the star points, place the balls as desired, and solder them to the points with hard solder (B). Use the chip method to place your solder chips at the joints before heating, and carefully solder the balls to the points. Pickle and dry the metal.

4 Using your needle files, clean up the edge of the sheet. Solder the bezel collar to the sheet using medium solder (C); make sure the solder chips are touching both the bezel wall and the back sheet when heated. For a cleaner joint, place the chips of solder inside the bezel collar. This will ensure less cleanup later on if the solder flows where you don't want it to go.

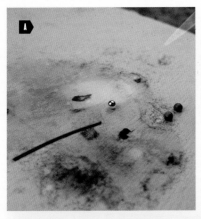

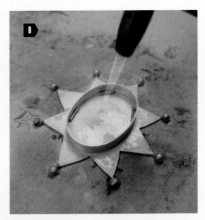

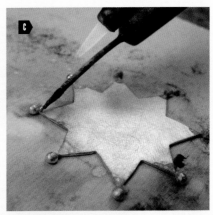

5 With chasing tools, add pattern to the star, taking care not to mar the sides of the bezel (D).

6 To create the pin spring, cut a length of 18-gauge silver wire approximately 3 inches long. Follow lesson 20 on page 135 to create the spring mechanism (E). Use easy solder, and be careful not to overheat your previous solder joints on the other side.

7 Do any cleanup needed, making sure the inside of the bezel cup is clean and dry. Then place the stone into the bezel and set (F), using the bezel roller, pusher, and burnisher as necessary and referring to lesson 17 on page 116 as needed.

8 Finish the piece as appropriate. I finished this brooch with a soft steel brush and dry green scrub pad, brushing the metal only to avoid damaging the fragile turquoise. Be sure to take into account the fragility of your stone when finishing the metal to avoid scratching or chipping the stone's surface.

PROJECT

GRAPE LEAF EARRINGS

This project uses 4mm round beads, piercing, forming, and a basic wire-wrapping technique that will be familiar to those who have used wire-wrapping as a cold connection. The beads are connected to jump rings linked in a chain, descending from leaf elements. Wire "pins" are threaded through the beads and jump ring chain. They are made by heating segments of fine-silver wire until the tips melt into a ball. Fine-silver wire is softer than sterling, allowing for easier wrapping. If you do not have any on hand, use sterling silver wire. Heating the wire to ball its end will anneal and soften the metal.

I used 4mm semiprecious peridot gemstone beads for the "grapes," but these earrings also look great when made with pearls or multicolored beads. A shape template for the leaves can be found on page 154.

Finished sterling silver and peridot earrings. **PHOTO BY ALLEN BRYAN**

WHAT YOU'LL NEED

**Essential workbench tools
(see page 22)**

**Basic soldering tool kit
(see page 23)**

**Sterling silver sheet metal,
22 gauge**

Jeweler's saw

Drill bits, 1mm and 2mm

Dapping block

Dapping punches

**Sterling silver round wire,
24 and 19 gauge**

**Fine-silver round wire,
26–28 gauge**

**45 beads or gemstones
of any shape, 3–4mm**

Needle-nose pliers

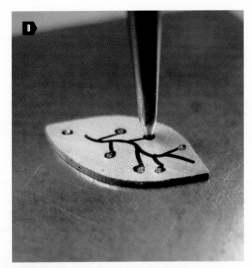

1. Using the leaf template on page 154 and your jeweler's saw, cut out eight leaves from the 22-gauge sheet (A). File the leaf edges with a needle file to remove any roughness, burrs, and saw marks.

2. To embellish your leaves with a pierced pattern, use the template again to copy the vein pattern onto each leaf. You'll be using the round ends of the veins as entry points for your drill bit, so make divots on those spots with a center punch for easier drilling (B).

3. Working over a wood block and using the 1mm drill bit, drill holes through the leaves at each divot. Use a 2mm drill bit to drill a hole at the top of each leaf; this hole is for adding the connecting jump rings. Redraw any vein lines that may have disappeared during the drilling process.

4. On each leaf, insert the saw blade through one of the holes, and cut along the vein lines carefully (C). You'll have to remove the blade at times and enter the leaves from different holes to cut the entire design in each one. After all piercing is completed, sand all the leaf surfaces with 400-grit sandpaper, removing any unwanted marks or scratches.

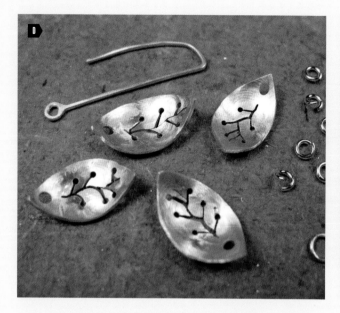

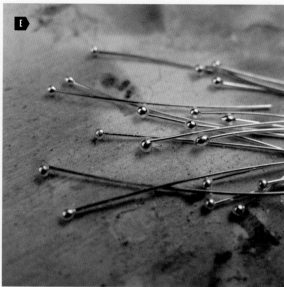

5 To create the curve in the leaves, place each one (one at a time) into a large depression in the dapping block, and curve them slightly with a corresponding punch. Alternately, you can form the curve in the leaf by using a round mandrel and rawhide hammer. Tap the leaf lightly against the mandrel until you have the desired shape.

6 Make jump rings from the 24-gauge wire to connect the components (see lesson 5 on page 43 if needed). There are four 4mm jump rings for connecting the leaves (two for each earring) and sixteen 2.5mm jump rings for connecting the beads and making the earring wire (eight for each earring). Use the small handle of a needle file, a nail, or a dapping tool as a mandrel to form the jump rings.

   Then make French earring wires from two 2-inch segments of 19-gauge wire, and file one end on each of the wires flat. Solder the wires to two of the small jump rings to make the connecting loop; when doing this, position the jump ring opening where the wire will connect to it, and close it. After pickling and drying, use half-round pliers to bend the wire at a point 1 inch up from the jump ring. Lightly hammer the earring wire with a chasing hammer to flatten and harden it.

   At this point you should have four leaves, two large jump rings, eight small jump rings, and one earring wire for each earring (D).

7 To make the pins that go through the beads, cut forty-five 1½-inch segments from the fine-silver wire. Using your torch, carefully ball one end of each wire, and set them aside to cool (E). The balls need to be big enough not to slip through the bead hole. If using sterling wire, you'll have to pickle the pins; fine-silver wires will be clean and ready to use.

8 Now you're ready to assemble the leaf elements and jump rings on the French earring wires. Use needle-nose pliers to open and close the jump rings. Start with one earring, and thread one leaf onto one of the 6mm jump rings through the top hole, concave sides facing out (hollowed sides out). Add the French wire and another leaf, also concave side out, and close the jump ring. This is the top of your earring. Thread the second 6mm jump ring through the first jump ring between the leaves on the opposite side from the French wire, and add the second set of leaves, threading them through their holes with the convex sides facing out. Close the jump ring. Add the remaining eight 3mm jump rings to the second 6mm jump ring between the second leaf pieces, connecting each one to each other in a continuous chain (F). Repeat these steps for the other earring.

9 Beads will now be added to the eight-jump-ring chain. Each small jump ring has two "sides" that I refer to here. To better understand this, hold one of the earrings by its French wire so that all the jump rings and leaves fall downward. Look at the small jump ring chain and note how the rings are linked to one another, alternating the front view of one ring and the side view, repeating all the way down (G). The "sides" of each jump ring are the east/west areas of the rings between the upper and lower connecting rings. This is where the beads will be connected.

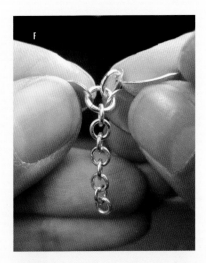

10 The first 3mm jump ring (closest to the second leaf element) has four beads, two on each side. To create the connecting loop for the first bead, insert one of the balled-wire segments through the bead's hole, and thread the wire through one side of the first small jump ring. With your fingers, make a small loop with the wire by bending the wire back to the top of the bead. Wrap the wire around itself at least three times; this should look like a tiny noose (H). Snip off the excess wire from the end (more than 1mm) with flush cutters. Gently squeeze the snipped wire end with needle-nose pliers to secure it and make a smooth connection. Add another bead to the same side of the jump ring. Then do the same for the other side (for four beads total, two on each side).

11 Continue down the jump ring chain; the second, third, and fourth 3mm jump rings should all be the same, having four beads (two on each side). For the fifth, sixth, and seventh jump rings, add only two beads (one on each side). The eighth (bottom) jump ring has only one bead that will dangle at the bottom. The beads should look like a cone-shaped cluster of grapes. Repeat this process with the other earring.

12 To finish the earrings, brush the metal gently with a brass brush, dish soap, and warm water.

GEAR NECKLACE

This project requires some skill and attention to detail. It incorporates flush-set stones, and flush setting can be a tough process to master. Practicing with small, nonprecious stones and metal is a good idea until you have confidence with this technique. Be sure the metal into which the stones will be set is thicker than the height of the stones to create a deep enough seat for them. Cut the seats for the stones carefully. Check the fit often, being careful not to overcut. A shape template for this project is located on page 154.

The sterling silver element in this piece has been oxidized and polished with a brass brush. As I've done here, you can string the pendants on an 18-inch chain or cord of your choice. **PHOTO BY ALLEN BRYAN**

WHAT YOU'LL NEED

Essential workbench tools (see page 22)

Basic soldering tool kit (see page 23)

Reticulated sterling silver sheet metal, 18 gauge

Brass sheet, any gauge

Round tubing, 4mm

Easy solder

Drill bit, 1mm

Small faceted stones, 2mm

90° hart burr

Setting tools

Liver of sulfur (optional)

1 To create reticulated silver sheet, follow lesson 14 on page 93. Using the small gear template, cut out the small gear shape from your reticulated silver with a jeweler's saw. Clean up your edges with needle files, removing all burrs and saw marks. Using the large gear template, cut a large gear shape out of the brass sheet. As with the small gear shape, clean up the metal as needed (A).

2 To create the bails for the gears, cut two small slices of the round tubing approximately 2mm long. Solder one to what will now be the top segment of each gear using easy solder (B). Pickle and dry your metals.

3 After doing any needed cleanup with sandpaper, decide where you want to place the stones. Mark the spots, and drill small holes through the metal. The holes should be smaller than the diameter of the stones to be set.

4 Following lesson 18 on page 118, flush-set the stones using the 90° hart burr and setting tools (C).

5 Clean up the setting marks around the stones if needed. I lightly sanded around the stones with 400-grit sandpaper.

6 Oxidize the silver gear with liver of sulfur if desired. Finish the metals with a soapy, wet brass brush. Rub the brass gear with a green scrub pad for a matte surface and added contrast between the pieces.

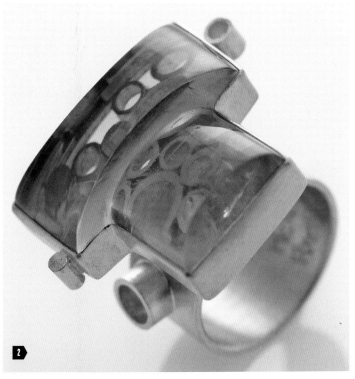

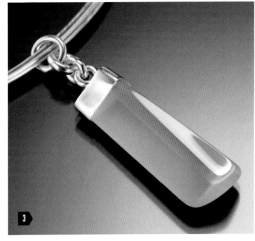

GALLERY
STONES & BEADS

1. PIN BY TAMI RODRIG

sterling silver, paint, beads, paper, and resin

Nonprecious elements are set in resin in this pin.
Photo by Robert Diamante

2. BERYL RING BY MELISSA FINELLI

sterling silver, 18K gold, and beryl

The uncommon shape of the bezel-set beryl stone
makes this piece truly unique. *Photo by Peter Harris*

3. PENDANT BY LAURA PRESHONG

sterling silver and glass

The glass element hangs from a sterling silver bezel
setting in this elegant pendant. *Photo by Allen Bryan*

4. JESTER NECKLACE BY JENNIFER CHIN

sterling silver and peridot

The semiprecious peridot stones in this necklace are
held in sterling silver bezel settings. The backs of each
bezel are open to allow light through each setting, giving
the faceted stones more luster. *Photo by Allen Bryan*

6

ADVANCED
TECHNIQUES

FORM & FUNCTION: BASIC MECHANISMS

Mechanisms in jewelry are used to attach, hold, fasten, and suspend components. Commercially created mechanisms are called *findings* and include clasps, earring wires, nuts, cuff link backs, and pin backs. Premade findings are convenient, but creating your own mechanisms will add a completed look to your jewelry, and this chapter will include lessons on these essential jewelry-making techniques.

Creating basic mechanisms, such as clasps, hinges, and latches is a way to add function to a piece. These elements can add elaborate decoration or be invisible; a mechanism's design depends on your intention. Many handmade mechanisms are engineering puzzles, a challenge for a jeweler looking for a way to connect two pieces. And the mechanism itself is often the focal point of a piece.

The following two lessons, like the rest of the lessons in this chapter, build on the basic fabrication and soldering skills learned previously. Be sure to practice the lessons with nonprecious metals to get a feel for each technique.

CIRCLE HOOP EARRINGS BY JULIA GROOS, *sterling silver*

These sterling silver hoop earrings use a riveted hinge mechanism for opening and closing. **PHOTO BY FREDRICK LEE**

ROYAL NECKLACE BY JENNIFER CHIN, *sterling silver*

This necklace has a simple clasp that incorporates smoothly with the design of the necklace; it is both functional and decorative. **PHOTO BY ALLEN BRYAN**

Various commercially made findings, including cuff link backs, earring wires, clips, and jump rings.

CLASPS

Closing mechanisms can be the most challenging to create. Whether decorative, purely functional, or even invisible (such as a pin back), they must always be well made, secure, and easy to use. Commercial clasps are widely available and practical, but a handmade clasp is less likely to interfere with a design and adds a refined element to your jewelry. A handmade clasp shows that you considered the piece as a whole from beginning to end.

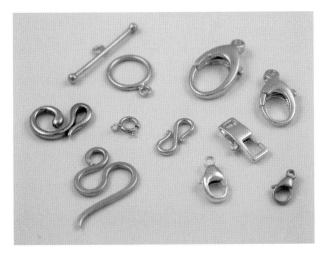

Clockwise from top left: various clasps, including commercially made toggle, lobster, and S clasps and assorted handmade S clasps.

Pin backs can be either solely functional, like the far one in this image, or designed to have a decorative flair, like the near example.

BRACELET BY TAMI RODRIG, *sterling silver, paint, paper, and resin*

The toggle clasp is fully incorporated into the design of this bracelet. The clasp itself has the same construction and interest as the other bracelet elements but with function, making it an interesting focal point of the piece.
PHOTO BY ROBERT DIAMANTE

POM-POM BRACELET BY JENNIFER CHIN, *sterling silver and 14K gold*

An S clasp is the closing mechanism here.
PHOTO BY ALLEN BRYAN

LESSON 19 ⟩ MAKING A BASIC S CLASP

The most simple and basic clasp is an S clasp. Excellent for necklaces and bracelets, an S clasp is created with a few bends, using round-nose pliers. As they are so simple, embellishment can make this clasp very special—even turning it into the focal point of a piece. Wire used for an S clasp can be forged to create pointed or curled ends, it can be hammered at its rounded points, and its end can also be balled using heat from a torch.

WHAT YOU'LL NEED

Essential workbench tools (see page 22)
Basic soldering tool kit (see page 23)
Annealed round wire, 12–18 gauge
Round-nose pliers

1 Cut a length of wire, and with round-nose pliers, bend the end into a U shape.

2 Bring the round-nose pliers about 1 inch from the U shape, and bend the wire around the thicker part of the pliers to create the first curve of the S shape. Then move the pliers again to create the second curve of the S shape. It can be helpful to use two pairs of round-nose pliers to form even, rounded curves. To create curled ends, bend each ending point of the S shape with the round-nose pliers into a small U shape.

3 With pliers or your fingers, squeeze one side of the S so that the wires touch. Use a small (1mm) chip of hard solder to solder the section where the wires meet.

4 Either sand the ends to taper them, or use the torch to slightly ball the ends with heat.

LESSON 20 ▶ MAKING A SPRING PIN BACK LATCH

A spring pin back latch is a simple and beautiful mechanism consisting of a pin stem and a latch that are created from one piece of wire. The mechanism is made by soldering a long U-shaped segment of wire onto the back side of a brooch. The U shape is then cut so that a small segment of wire remains on one side of the brooch, while the other side has the remaining length. The latch is created by bending the shorter segment of wire into a small U, leaving space for the pin stem to slide into it. The longer length of wire is the pin stem, which is formed with round pliers into a coil at its base. The bending of the pin stem into a coiled spring causes the metal to work-harden and become springy. This tension created from the work-hardened coil allows the pin to be held in the latch.

When placing a pin mechanism on a brooch, it's important to consider how the piece will hang when worn. A pin back placed in the middle or too low on the back side of a top-heavy brooch may cause the piece to fall forward. A pin back placed approximately three-quarters of the way up the back of the brooch will hold the pin's weight evenly. The following practice lesson uses brass with a sterling silver pin stem and latch.

WHAT YOU'LL NEED

Essential workbench tools (see page 22)

Basic soldering tool kit (see page 23)

Silver wire, 18 gauge

Sheet metal

Round-nose pliers

2 Holding the wire in locking tweezers, solder the flush ends to the back of the brooch with easy solder. Medium or hard solder may be used if there are no previously soldered components in the brooch. Pickle and dry the piece. Clean up any excess solder on the back.

Cut the wire about ½ inch from one of the solder joints. Clean up the end with files and sandpaper, and bend the wire into a small half-circle shape, as shown. This will be the latch side.

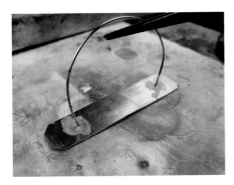

1 Cut a section of wire that is approximately 1 inch longer than the width of the "brooch" (remember, we're using a plain piece of sheet metal for practice here). File both ends flush. Bend the wire into a wide U shape so that both ends touch down on the far sides of the brooch. The ends should be level, flush against the metal, and at least 3mm from the edges.

3 The other side is the pin wire. Create a springlike loop with round-nose pliers by wrapping the wire one turn around the pliers.

4 Snip the end of the pin stem if it extends farther than a few millimeters past the latch. File the end into a sharp point with a hand file, and remove any unintentional marks from all surfaces with 400-grit sandpaper.

HINGES

Hinges are mechanisms that allow swiveling action at a joint. They're excellent for connecting links and providing movement. Similar to rivets, most hinges are constructed with tubing and wire. They can be hidden, have inner springs, or even serve as clasps.

LESSON 21 — MAKING A BASIC HINGE

This lesson is for the most basic hinge, a very useful mechanism for jewelers.

OSTRICH CUFFS BY JULIA GROOS, *sterling silver and ostrich leather*

These bracelets use hinged closing mechanisms and locking pins made from sterling sliver to open and clasp them shut.
PHOTO BY FREDRICK LEE

WHAT YOU'LL NEED

Essential workbench tools (see page 22)

Basic soldering tool kit (see page 23)

Sheet metal of your choice, 18 gauge or thicker

Tubing in small diameter, approximately 2.5mm

Steel rod that fits perfectly inside tubing (drill bits or nails work well)

Sterling silver wire to fit inner diameter of tubing snugly

1 To prepare your sheet metal, cut two pieces that are each 1 inch square, and file the edges smooth and straight.

2 With a round needle file, file a round groove into one edge of each sheet (A). This is where the tubing will lie. Use a ring clamp or vise to secure the metal and ensure even filing.

3 Decide how many pieces of tubing you want for your hinge, and cut it with a saw and tube cutter (B). A hinge should have an uneven number of tube segments to ensure the strength of the hinge and create a more balanced-looking result. (The hinge in this lesson uses five pieces of tubing.) File the tube edges, being careful to keep the edges straight.

4 Thread the pieces of tubing onto the steel rod in the order they will be soldered down. Be sure that they meet closely. Lay the metal sheets on your soldering surface, with the grooved edges facing each other. Place the tubing into the rounded grooves (C). Check that the tubing meets the grooves.

5 Place a small drop of flux in the middle of each segment on alternating sides of the tubing. Don't flux the entire piece, just in one spot at the alternating joints. This is to keep the solder from flowing through the entire hinge. Cut small pieces of hard solder chips. Turn on your torch, and use a small flame to heat the hinge. After the flux has stopped boiling, place the solder chips on each of the fluxed areas using your solder pick (D).

6 Slowly heat the entire piece, concentrating on the hinges until the solder flows (E). Don't let the solder flow all the way down the joint; just tack the tubing in place.

7 Let the piece cool, remove the steel rod, separate the metal sheets, and reflux the joint.

8 With the torch on a gentle flame, heat one of the sides until the solder flows through the entire joint. Repeat with the other segment, and then pickle both parts.

9 If needed, gently file the ends of the tubing on one piece of the sheet until they're flush with those on the adjoining sheet segment. Be careful not to overfile.

10 Reposition the segments together, and insert the silver wire through them. The wire should fit snugly inside the tubing. This is the pin that holds the hinges together. Cut the wire with your saw so that it extends about 1mm past each end.

11 Using your riveting hammer, gently flare and rivet the ends of each wire (F). The hinge should move easily. Be careful not to overhammer the ends, as the hinge segments can be damaged and affect the hinge's ability to swivel back and forth. Sand with 400-grit sandpaper.

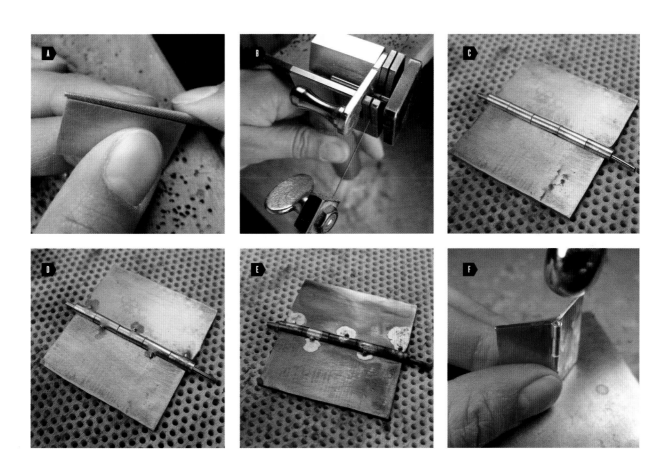

MIXING METALS

Mixing different types of metals in a piece is a way to add interesting, multicolored detail and more complex design. Inlay techniques using different-colored metals or solder can result in unique, delicate results, as well. The following lessons and projects combine silver, copper, and brass and require an intermediate level of soldering skill, as there can be many heating operations in a single piece.

Marriage of metals, sometimes called *puzzle inlay*, is one method of mixing metals that uses positive and negative space with two or more different-colored metals. Another way of mixing metals into a pattern is to solder different strips or shapes together, cutting and resoldering for added detail. The result is an interesting multicolored sheet metal that can be dapped, formed, and soldered as desired.

NECKLACE BY MELISSA FINELLI, *sterling silver and 18K gold*

The inlay in this necklace was created using sterling silver and gold wire. Holes were drilled through sterling silver sheet into which gold wire was inserted and soldered. After the ends of the wires were filed and sanded flush to the sheet, the shape was formed, and the entire piece was oxidized to bring out the inlay pattern. The hinge mechanisms use segments of balled wire held by loops to create a chain of interesting movable links. **PHOTO BY PETER HARRIS**

LESSON 22

MARRIAGE OF METALS

As mentioned previously, marriage of metals is an inlay technique used to join different-colored metals together as one. An inlay design is created using a puzzlelike method to assemble the metals, with positive and negative space. In this lesson, one metal is cut and used as a nesting shape to fill in the same shape that has been removed in another piece of metal. Think of it as placing a single puzzle piece into a puzzle; the piece should fit snugly into the space like it belongs there. The two different metals are then soldered together to form one solid sheet.

WHAT YOU'LL NEED

**Essential workbench tools
(see page 22)**

**Basic soldering tool kit
(see page 23)**

**Contrasting-color sheet metals
of your choice, each 22 gauge**

Hard solder

❶ Draw or scribe a shape on the sheet metal that will be the outer area of your inlay design. If you've drawn your design on a piece of paper, transfer it to the metal, following the instructions for using templates found on page 154.

❷ Pierce out the inner area of the design by drilling a hole in that area to create an entry for your saw and then carefully sawing out your shape. Clean up the edges with a needle file, filing any rough spots or burrs.

❸ Place the background shape on top of the metal to be inlaid, and draw or scribe the shape of the negative space on the inlay metal (A). Be sure to make a clear mark.

❹ Cut out the shape, cutting just outside the scribed line. (If the shape is too large, you can file it down later, but if the shape is too small, you'll have to recut it.)

❺ Check the fit with the background piece, and file and reshape as needed. Be careful not to overfile; the fit should be snug, with no space in between the metals.

❻ Place your metals on the soldering board, and flux all around the cut-out shape. Heat and stick solder the two pieces together with hard solder (B). The solder should fill the entire seam. Flux and resolder if there are any gaps.

❼ After pickling and drying, remove excess solder from the sheet with sandpaper (C).

   Note: Doming the sheet is sometimes helpful for removing excess solder. The sheet can be reflattened after solder has been removed using a rawhide hammer. With the convex side up, hammer the dome gently against a steel plate until it's flat. Be sure to use medium and easy solders during any subsequent heating to ensure the integrity of your inlay.

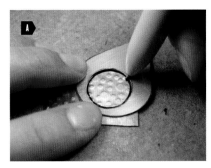

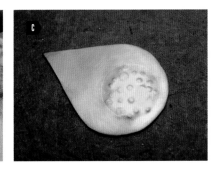

SOLDER INLAY

Solder inlay—in which you use solder to contrast with the metal in your piece—creates subtle and delicate two-toned surface designs. There are many ways to achieve this, one of which is with a jeweler's saw: The saw blade cuts the design in the metal into which solder is flowed. Thinner saw blades result in thinner lines of solder; larger blades result in thicker lines.

Another way to add contrasting-colored solder to metal is by flowing solder into any sort of depression on the surface of the metal. Filed marks, divots, embossing, and stamped designs work well with this technique. After solder is flowed into a depression, the surface is sanded to remove excess solder, revealing the design in solder. Experiment and see what you come up with. Solder inlay is a great way to add beautiful, one-of-a-kind detail.

CUFF BRACELET BY JENNIFER CHIN, *copper and silver solder*

I created the design on this bracelet using a solder inlay technique. Using metal stamps, I stamped the shapes onto the surface of the copper and then flowed hard silver solder into the depressions. Excess solder was sanded away to reveal the shapes colored by the contrasting silver solder. The bracelet is hinged on one side to open and close it. The clasp mechanism was created similarly to the hinge, using tubing. A removable pin closes the bracelet. **PHOTO BY ALLEN BRYAN**

ADVANCED TECHNIQUES

CREATING SOLDER INLAY

This is a basic lesson in creating solder inlay in metal. Always choose a solder that's different in color from the metal being used, for best results. For brass and copper, use hard silver solder. For sterling silver, use hard gold solder to achieve contrasting detail. Oxidizing sterling silver with gold solder inlay will create interesting results, as the gold solder won't be affected by the oxidation.

WHAT YOU'LL NEED

Essential workbench tools (see page 22)
Basic soldering tool kit (see page 23)
Copper or brass sheet metal, 24 gauge
Hard silver wire solder

1 Begin by drawing a design on your sheet metal (or transferring it onto the metal from paper). Your drawing can touch the edge of the metal to allow the saw to enter with a simple cut, or if it doesn't (like the design pictured here), you'll have to drill a tiny hole (or holes) in the design through the sheet (in the interior of the design) to create the saw entry point. Be sure the design doesn't cut the metal apart; the sheet needs to remain in one piece for the soldering to be effective and even.

2 Saw the lines of the drawing using saw blades that correspond to the thickness of the lines in your design. I used a 0/2 blade to create my design. Once the design is completely cut, lay the sheet on the soldering board, and flux the sawed lines. Begin to heat the metal with your torch.

3 Using the stick-soldering technique (see page 55), flow solder into the lines. Be sure it fills each line entirely.

4 Pickle and dry the sheet, and clean up excess solder with files and sandpaper.

LAMINATION INLAY

Lamination inlay is a simple process that uses a rolling mill to combine two metals. Sheets of different metals are soldered together and then rolled until they are flush. One sheet of metal should be thick (22 gauge) and the other thin (26 gauge). The thicker sheet is used as the base onto which the thinner metal is soldered. The thinner metal is flattened against the thicker metal when it's rolled through the rolling mill, and the resulting thickness is thinner than the original heavier-gauged sheet. This technique also allows for a more organic effect than marriage of metals, as designs soldered and rolled through a mill will be compressed, their original shapes distorted.

LESSON 24 — CREATING LAMINATION INLAY

This lesson uses sheet metal, but along with sheet, thin slices of wire and tubing can create interesting patterns; just keep in mind that their shapes will be distorted after going through the mill. Whatever types of metals you're using, make sure that they're of contrasting color to create the inlay design. I used 7mm sterling silver circles on a copper sheet here.

WHAT YOU'LL NEED

Essential workbench tools (see page 22)
Basic soldering tool kit (see page 23)
Sheet metal in different colors, 22 and 26 gauge
Hard solder
Rolling mill

1. Cut the inlay shapes from the thinner sheet metal. Cut the thicker sheet for the bottom as desired.

2. Clean the cut-out shapes, lay them on the soldering board, and apply flux to the upward-facing sides of the shapes. One at a time, heat the cut-out shapes and place a moderate amount of solder (I used 3mm chips for my 7mm circles) onto the surface of each shape (A). Flow the solder onto the backs. Be careful not to overheat; you just want the solder to flow (see sweat soldering on page 56).

3 After the solder has flowed, allow the cut-out shapes to cool slightly before pickling. Rinse and dry them after they're pickled and clean.

4 Place the bottom sheet metal on the soldering board, and flux the entire surface; then lay your cut-out shapes on top, solder side down. Heat the metals until the shapes are completely soldered down (B). Keep in mind that the thicker bottom sheet will need more heat, and the cut-outs will heat faster. Allow the metal to cool, and then pickle.

5 After pickling and drying, roll the metal through the rolling mill (C). Anneal the metal before making another pass through the mill.

6 Sand and use the patterned metal as desired (D).

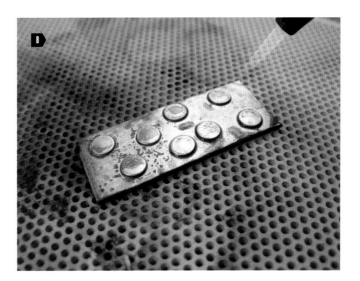

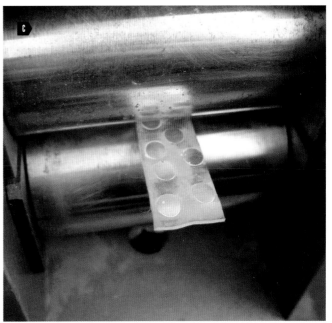

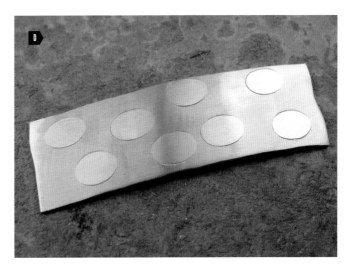

DOMED CIRCLE PENDANT

This projects uses lamination inlay and dapping to create a simple pendant. The surface design can be embellished or simplified. Experiment with wire and sheet in your rolling mill, and see what you can make. I oxidized the pendant to bring out the gold detail. String the pendant on a thin gold or oxidized sterling silver chain.

Here, 14K gold tubing is inlaid in sterling silver to create the circle designs. **PHOTO BY ALLEN BRYAN**

ADVANCED TECHNIQUES

WHAT YOU'LL NEED

Essential workbench tools (see page 22)

Basic soldering tool kit (see page 23)

3mm 14K gold tubing

Sterling silver sheet metal, 22 gauge

Hard, medium, and easy solder

Rolling mill

Dapping block

Dapping punches

1 Cut eight 2mm-long segments of 14K gold tubing. Remove any burrs.

2 Lay your sterling silver sheet onto the soldering board, and flux the areas where the tubing will be placed. Place the tubing in the desired pattern. I arranged my tubing in a loose pattern, four pieces in a square shape on a slight diagonal with the other four pieces mirroring it. Place tiny chips of hard solder inside each tube. Heat and solder the tubes to the sheet (A). Pickle and dry the metal.

3 Run the sheet through the rolling mill until the tubes are flush with the surface of the sheet (B). You'll probably have to reanneal the sheet after every two passes through the rolling mill. I rolled my sheet four times (annealed twice) through the mill to achieve this result.

4 Decide where to remove the pattern from your inlaid sheet. Cut out two 1-inch circles from the sheet, and file the edges. Place each circle, one at a time, into your dapping block, and shape it into a dome (C).

5 Sand the edges of the domes until they are flush when held together with domed sides out.

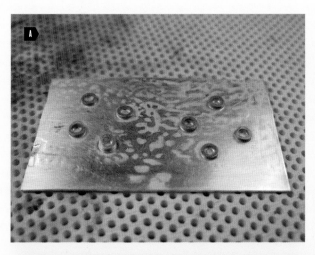

6 Using steel binding wire (thin steel wire), bind the domes together so that they're secure and won't pop apart when heated (D). Flux the seam where the two domes meet. The edges should meet each other perfectly, with no space between them. Solder the seam completely closed around the entire piece with medium solder, allow to cool, and then pickle. Remember to remove the steel binding wire from the piece before pickling.

7 Check the seam for any holes, and resolder if necessary. Clean up the seam with needle files, removing any excess solder and making the seam invisible. Sand the piece with 400-grit sandpaper.

8 Use a small slice of sterling silver tubing or a jump ring to create the bail, and solder it to the top with easy solder (E).

9 To finish, oxidize the metal, and brush all the surfaces with a brass brush to shine.

PROJECT
BIRD BROOCH

This project uses the marriage-of-metals technique to create a stylized checkerboard pattern in the bird's wing. The details of a checkerboard pattern like this can be as intricate as you want; just be cautious of previously soldered joints when heating. Shape templates for this project can be found on page 154.

This sterling silver, copper, brass, and 14K gold brooch combines a few techniques from previous chapters. Riveting is used decoratively to create the bird's eye and functionally as a mechanism to connect the wing. Marriage of metals creates the pattern on the wing, and a spring pin back latch makes the brooch wearable. **PHOTO BY ALLEN BRYAN**

WHAT YOU'LL NEED

Essential workbench tools (see page 20)

Basic soldering tool kit (see page 21)

Silver, copper, and brass sheet metals, 22 gauge

Hard, medium, and easy solder

Sterling silver wire, 20 gauge

3mm tubing of your choice

1 To create a patterned sheet for the bird's wing, cut out four ½ x 2-inch segments from both the silver and brass sheet metal, plus two in copper. Use your jeweler's saw for this, and then file the edges flush.

2 Arrange the pieces on your soldering board, alternating types, and solder the pieces together with hard solder. Use the stick-solder method for ease of soldering and less cleanup (A). Pickle and dry the metal.

3 To create a checkerboard pattern, cut the sheet apart, and solder the pieces together in an alternating arrangement using medium solder. (If desired, repeat this process; cutting thinner and thicker pieces will create more intricate pattern detail.)

4 Using the bird-wing template, cut out the shape from your checkerboard sheet using the jeweler's saw (B). Clean up your sheet, filing the edges clean of burrs and saw marks and then sanding it to remove excess solder and bring out the checker-board pattern. If there's a lot of excess solder to remove, use a split-mandrel attachment with sandpaper on your flexible shaft to make this job easier.

5 Using the bird template on page 154, cut out the shape from a new piece of sterling silver sheet (C). File and sand the edges as desired.

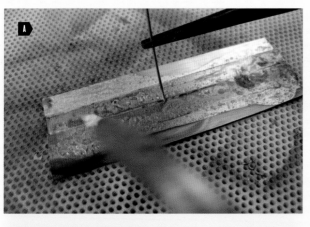

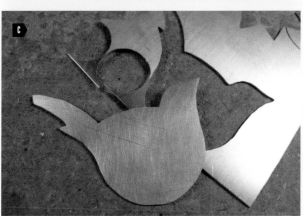

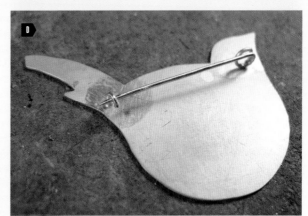

6 Create the pin back on the back of the bird shape using the 20-gauge sterling silver wire (D). (See lesson 20 on page 135 if needed.) After soldering, pickle and dry the metal.

7 The eye and the wing attachment are both created with rivets (E). To create the eye, make a decorative rivet with the tubing (see lesson 8 on page 48 if needed). Attach the wing with a wire rivet made from the 20-gauge wire (see lesson 7 on page 46 if needed).

8 To finish, use a steel brush and green scrub pad to create a brushed surface.

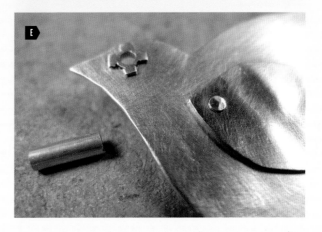

PROJECT
EMBOSSED LOCKET

This is a great project combining the techniques of embossing and soldering and employing hinge mechanisms. The locket is a basic box with a swiveling, hinged side for opening and closing. The latch side uses the same hinge idea but with a removable pin to keep the locket securely shut. There are more than three soldering operations in this piece, so careful heating is required to avoid reflowing previously soldered joints.

The finished sterling silver locket can hold pictures or be a reliquary for special objects. To further embellish the piece, cut a decorative window opening out of the front panel to allow a view inside the locket.
PHOTO BY ALLEN BRYAN

WHAT YOU'LL NEED

Essential workbench tools (see page 22)

Basic soldering tool kit (see page 23)

Sterling silver sheet metal, 22 gauge

Hard, medium, and easy solder

Broken saw blades (for embossing pattern)

Rolling mill

3mm tubing of your choice

Silver wire, 16 gauge

1 Cut a strip 3 inches x 6mm out of the sterling silver sheet metal. This will be the wall of the locket. File the edges straight and even with a flat hand file, clamping the metal into a bench vise for straighter edges and ease of filing.

2 Bend the strip around a mandrel until the ends meet, solder the ends together with hard solder, and then pickle and dry the strip.

3 Reshape this metal ring into a round shape by hammering it lightly while it's around a mandrel using a rawhide hammer. Gently squeeze the ring in your hand to form an oval shape (A).

4 Sand the edges of the oval ring so that they are flat and even. To do this, lay 220-grit sandpaper on your working surface and move the ring over it gently in a figure-eight motion. Do this on both sides.

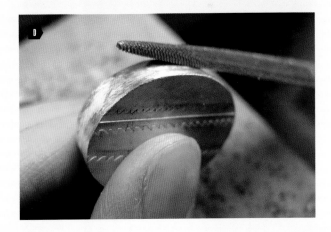

5 Anneal the metal that will serve as the front and back panels of the locket, and emboss it with the rolling mill (B). Use large, broken saw blades to create the design. Make sure to use enough sheet for the front and back of your locket, and remember to use brass or copper sheet to protect your rollers when using ferrous metal to emboss.

6 After flattening the embossed sheet with a rawhide mallet, decide where you'd like to remove the pattern. Cut out two segments, one for the front and one for the back locket panels. Be sure to cut out segments that are large enough to accommodate the oval ring. Allow for at least 2mm of extra metal around the oval for ease of soldering.

7 Place one of the patterned sheets (pattern side down) on the soldering board. Flux the entire sheet, and place the oval ring on the sheet. Solder the ring onto the sheet using medium solder (C). Place the solder around the outside perimeter of the oval, making sure the solder chips touch the bottom of the oval's wall and the sheet. Pickle and dry the metal.

8 Using the jeweler's saw, cut around the oval ring, removing the excess sheet. Repeat steps 7 and 8 on the other side of the oval to create a completely closed box.

9 File the sides along the seams until the edges are flush and the seams are invisible (D). Sand with 220-grit sandpaper to remove the file marks.

10 Scribe or draw a line around the wall of the locket at the exact center. To make this easier, use a ruler to find the midpoint of the wall, making marks every quarter of an inch. Connect the marks by scribing or drawing lines between them (E). Following the line, cut the locket in half with a frame saw. Make sure to take your time and cut carefully.

11 After the two pieces are separated, lightly sand the cut edges, and line up the locket pieces, making sure they're flush. Use binding wire or tape to "reconnect" them (i.e., hold them together).

12 Create a seat for the hinge using a round-needle file (see lesson 21 on page 136 if needed). Begin by filing a ½-inch groove in the center of one of the longer sides of the oval. You want to remove enough metal that your hinge will sit in alignment but not so much that the edge becomes too thin. Repeat the same process on the other side to make a ½-inch groove; this will be the latch side.

13 To create the sections of your hinge, cut a 12mm segment of tubing. Cut this again into three smaller sections, one 6mm piece and two 3mm pieces for a stronger hinge. File them flush so that they fit together evenly. Thread them onto a thin piece of steel wire, with the two smaller segments positioned on the ends. Place this into the ½-inch groove, and solder the sections into place with easy solder (F). The two outer segments should be soldered to the back of the locket, while the center tube is soldered to the front.

14 Repeat the process in step 13 for the latch side, but cut a ¼-inch segment of tubing and divide it into two 1mm pieces and one 4mm piece. Solder again with easy solder, making sure to solder the two outer segments to the back of the locket and the middle segment to the front.

As you're performing multiple soldering jobs with easy solder, be careful to keep your flame away from the previously soldered hinge joint on the other side. After pickling and drying, check the fit of the hinges, which should be lined up perfectly. Insert wire into the hinges to check the positioning.

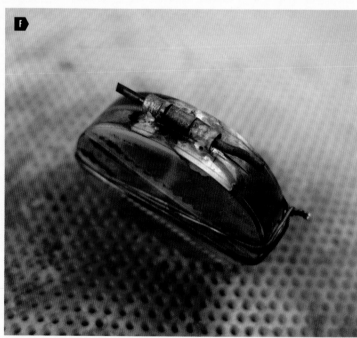

15 Make a jump ring for the top of the locket, and solder its opening shut with hard solder. Use a flat-needle file to file flat one side of the jump ring's edge. This will create a neater joint between the locket and the jump ring. Secure the locket in one pair of locking tweezers and the jump ring in another. Cut a chip of easy solder, and solder the jump ring to the back half of the locket by picking up the solder with the jump ring, letting the solder flow onto its flat surface, and then placing it onto the locket and flowing the solder again (G).

16 Rivet the hinge of the locket using the 16-gauge wire, making sure the hinge is easily movable and not too tight. Be careful to avoid hitting the surfaces surrounding the riveting area, as any unintentional hammer marks will have to be sanded later.

17 To create the lock for the latch side, you want to create a tiny pin that fits tightly into the tubing. For the top element, work over a flat soldering surface, and heat a ½-inch segment of the 16-gauge wire with your torch until it melts into a round ball (H). Pickle and dry the ball. Sand one side of the ball flat with 220-grit sandpaper to create an even soldering surface. Cut another segment of 16-gauge wire approximately 10mm long, and solder the wire to the flat side of the ball. Round the end of the wire as desired. The pin should fit snugly into the latch. If it seems too loose and can fall out, use a slightly thicker-gauge wire, and carefully file it smaller as necessary until it fits perfectly.

18 To finish the locket, sand all surfaces with 400-grit sandpaper. Shine with a steel brush.

2

3

GALLERY
ADVANCED TECHNIQUES

1. NECKLACE BY TAMI RODRIG

sterling silver, glass, beads, paper, paint, and resin

Note the toggle clasp closure here, which echoes the design of the main pendant element. *Photo by Robert Diamante*

2. AVOCADO CUFF NECKLACE

BY HILARY HACHEY

sterling silver

This interesting necklace has no clasp and is rigid. The hinges, located at several points along the back and sides, allow the segments to swivel open and closed. *Photo by Hap Sakwa*

3. MOSS & LICHEN NECKLACE

BY LAUREN SCHLOSSBERG

sterling silver and glass beads

This necklace of oxidized sterling silver components also makes use of a toggle clasp closure. *Photo by Hap Sakwa*

PROJECT TEMPLATES

To use the templates, trace the shapes onto tracing paper, cut them out, and tape them to whatever sheet metal you're using. Using a pencil or scribe, mark a line on the metal around the template shape. Remove the paper, and cut out the shape with your jeweler's saw.

To transfer the grape leaf element, trace or copy the image, and then cut it out and tape the shape to your metal. Draw or scribe the line around the leaf for your saw to follow. Using a center punch and hammer, create divots in the metal through the paper where the six dots are located. Remove the paper and cut out the grape leaf shape. Draw a connecting vein between the divots with a fine marker and then saw along those lines. Note that you can copy the template exactly or create your own design.

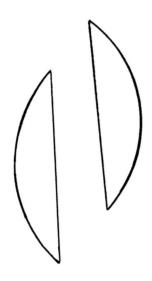

RETICULATED EARRINGS, page 104   **GRAPE LEAF EARRINGS,** page 122   **GEAR NECKLACE,** page 126

BIRD BROOCH (BIRD TEMPLATE), page 146   **BIRD BROOCH** (WING TEMPLATE), page 146

RING-SIZING GUIDE

This is a chart of American whole and half ring sizes and their measured size equivalents in millimeters and inches. Use it to figure out the inner diameter of a ring; for example, if you want to create a size 7 ring, your metal should measure 2 3/16 inches (54mm). A wide band (thicker than 1/4 inch) will require a larger size than the finger's measured size, as it needs to be roomier for a comfortable fit. Thicker rings should be made one quarter to one half size larger. Another consideration is knuckle size; if a ring cannot easily slide over the knuckle, the size should be increased. If you have large knuckles, measure the size of the knuckle, and use this measurement instead of the circumference of the base of the finger.

HOW TO MEASURE YOUR FINGER

1. Find a piece of string or a strip of paper no wider than 3/4 inch.

2. Wrap it around the base of the finger (or knuckle).

3. Use a pen to mark the spot where the paper or string overlaps and creates a complete circle.

4. Measure the string or paper with a ruler, from its starting end to the pen mark.

5. Using your measurement, find your size on the chart to the right.

RING SIZE CHART

RING SIZE	MEASURED SIZE IN INCHES	MEASURED SIZE IN MM
4	1 13/16	46.5
4.5	1 7/8	47.8
5	1 15/16	49
5.5	2	50.3
6	2 1/16	51.5
6.5	2 1/8	52.8
7	2 3/16	54
7.5	2 1/4	55.3
8	2 5/16	56.6
8.5	2 3/8	57.8
9	2 7/16	59.1
9.5	2 1/2	60.3
10	2 9/16	61.6
10.5	2 5/8	62.8
11	2 11/16	64.1
11.5	2 3/4	65.3
12	2 13/16	66.6
12.5	2 7/8	67.9
13	2 15/16	69.1

CIRCLE DIVIDER

A circle divider is a measurement tool used to dived a circle into uniform parts. You can also use it to trace and transfer perfect circles onto metal.

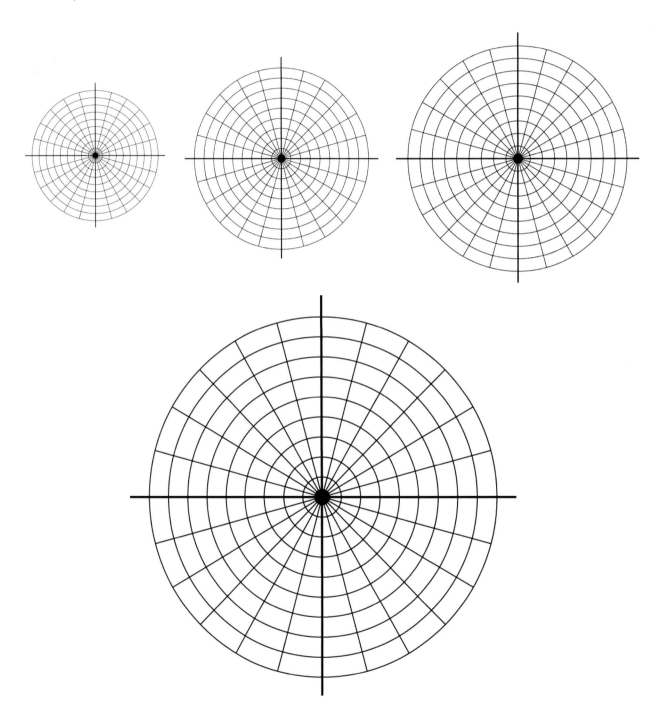

RESOURCES

MATERIALS AND EQUIPMENT SUPPLIERS

These vendors are resources for jewelry-making tools, raw materials, equipment, and casting. Casting, a jewelry manufacturing process not covered in this book, is a method of creating molds into which liquid metal is poured and solidified. The resulting object is called a casting. Used by many students, hobbyists, and professional jewelers, castings are usually created if fabrication by hand is difficult or too expensive. I've included my preferred casting company in this list as a future reference for beginning jewelers wanting to pursue design concepts with casting.

CRANSTON CASTING
Molding and casting.
www.cranstoncasting.com

GESSWEIN
Jewelers' tools, supplies, and equipment.
www.gesswein.com

HAUSER & MILLER CO.
Refining and precious metals.
www.hauserandmiller.com

HOOVER & STRONG
Precious metals and findings.
www.hooverandstrong.com

MYRON TOBACK
Findings and raw materials.
www.myrontoback.com

OTTO FREI
Jewelers' tools, supplies, and equipment.
www.OttoFrei.com

RIO GRANDE
Jewelers' tools, supplies, and equipment.
www.riogrande.com

STULLER
Jewelers' tools, supplies, and equipment.
www.stuller.com

ONLINE RESOURCES AND PUBLICATIONS

These publications and online resources are excellent references for the craft of jewelry making and are highly recommended for advice, inspiration, and support.

AMERICAN CRAFT COUNCIL
www.craftcouncil.org

AMERICAN CRAFT MAGAZINE
www.americancraftmag.org

AMERICAN STYLE MAGAZINE
www.americanstyle.com

ART JEWELRY MAGAZINE
www.artjewelrymag.com

BEAD&BUTTON MAGAZINE
www.beadandbutton.com

BEADWORK MAGAZINE
www.interweave.com/bead/beadwork_magazine/

THE CRAFTS REPORT
www.craftsreport.com

GANOSKIN
www.ganoskin.com

LAPIDARY JOURNAL JEWELRY ARTIST MAGAZINE
www.jewelryartistmagazine.com

METALSMITH MAGAZINE
www.snagmetalsmith.org

MJSA JOURNAL
A publication of the Manufacturing Jewelers & Suppliers of America.
www.mjsa.org/publications_and_information/mjsa_journal

ORNAMENT MAGAZINE
www.ornamentmagazine.com

SCHMUCK MAGAZIN
This is a great German magazine; *schmuck* is *jeweler* in German.
www.schmuckmagazin.de

SOCIETY OF ARTS AND CRAFTS
www.societyofcrafts.org

SOCIETY OF NORTH AMERICAN GOLDSMITHS
www.snagmetalsmith.org

STEP BY STEP WIRE JEWELRY MAGAZINE
www.stepbystepwire.com/wire/

CONTRIBUTING ARTISTS

THERESA CARSON
www.theresacarson.com

LISA CROWDER
www.lisacrowder.com

DONNA D'AQUINO
www.donnadaquino.com

MELISSA FINELLI
www.mellefinellijewelry.com

JULIA GROOS
www.juliagroos.com

HILARY HACHEY
www.hilaryhachey.com

CHIHIRO MAKIO
www.314studio.com

LAURA PRESHONG
www.laurapreshong.com

TAMI RODRIG
www.happyartstudio.com

LAUREN SCHLOSSBERG
www.laurenschlossbergjewelry.com

PETRA SEIBERTOVA
www.etsy.com/shop/petrastore

DONNA VEVERKA
www.donnavjewelry.com

JAYE WOODSTOCK
www.jayewoodstock.com

METRIC CONVERSION CHART

INCHES TO CM		CM TO INCHES			
1/16	0.16	1	3/8	36	14 1/8
1/8	0.32	2	3/4	37	14 5/8
3/16	0.48	3	1 1/8	38	15
1/4	0.64	4	1 5/8	39	15 3/8
5/16	0.79	5	2	40	15 3/4
3/8	0.95	6	2 3/8	41	16 1/8
7/16	1.11	7	2 3/4	42	16 1/2
1/2	1.27	8	3 1/8	43	16 7/8
9/16	1.43	9	3 1/2	44	17 1/4
5/8	1.59	10	4	45	17 3/4
11/16	1.75	11	4 3/8	46	18 1/8
3/4	1.91	12	4 3/4	47	18 1/2
13/16	2.06	13	5 1/8	48	18 7/8
7/8	2.22	14	5 1/2	49	19 1/4
15/16	2.38	15	5 7/8	50	19 5/8
1	2.54	16	6 1/4		
2	5.08	17	6 3/4		
3	7.65	18	7 1/8		
4	10.16	19	7 1/2		
5	12.70	20	7 7/8		
6	15.24	21	8 1/4		
7	17.78	22	8 5/8		
8	20.32	23	9		
9	22.66	24	9 1/2		
10	25.40	25	9 7/8		
11	27.94	26	10 1/4		
12	30.48	27	10 5/8		
13	33.02	28	11		
14	35.56	29	11 3/8		
15	38.10	30	11 7/8		
16	40.64	31	12 1/4		
17	43.18	32	12 5/8		
18	45.72	33	13		
19	48.26	34	13 3/8		
20	50.80	35	13 3/4		

ABOUT THE AUTHOR

Artist and metalsmith Jennifer Chin is the owner of Lush Metals, a jewelry studio whose designs are based on the idea of organic themes mixing with machine-inspired motifs, the interplay between these two extremes, and the beautiful and interesting mathematical patterns that occur in nature. She studied studio arts at the School of the Museum of Fine Arts in Boston. Her award-winning work can be seen at many fine crafts shows, museums, galleries, and boutiques throughout the United States and at www.lushmetals.com.

INDEX